NATIONS UNDER GOD

INTERNATIONAL THEOLOGICAL COMMENTARY

Fredrick Carlson Holmgren and George A. F. Knight
General Editors

Volumes now available

Genesis 1–11: From Eden to Babel
by Donald E. Gowan

Joshua: Inheriting the Land
by E. John Hamlin

Judges: At Risk in the Promised Land
by E. John Hamlin

1 Kings: Nations under God
by Gene Rice

Ezra and Nehemiah: Israel Alive Again
by Fredrick Carlson Holmgren

Song of Songs and Jonah: Revelation of God
by George A. F. Knight
and Friedemann W. Golka

Isaiah 1–39: The Lord Is Savior: Faith in National Crisis
by S. H. Widyapranawa

Isaiah 40–55: Servant Theology
by George A. F. Knight

Isaiah 56–66: The New Israel
by George A. F. Knight

Jeremiah 1–25: To Pluck Up, To Tear Down
by Walter Brueggemann

Daniel: Signs and Wonders
by Robert A. Anderson

Hosea: Grace Abounding
by H. D. Beeby

Joel and Malachi: A Promise of Hope, A Call to Obedience
by Graham S. Ogden
and Richard R. Deutsch

Amos and Lamentations: God's People in Crisis
by Robert Martin-Achard
and S. Paul Re'emi

Micah: Justice and Loyalty
by Juan I. Alfaro

Nahum, Obadiah, and Esther: Israel among the Nations
by Richard J. Coggins
and S. Paul Re'emi

Habakkuk and Zephaniah: Wrath and Mercy
by Mária Eszenyei Széles

Haggai and Zechariah: Rebuilding with Hope
by Carroll Stuhlmueller, C.P.

Forthcoming in 1991

Deuteronomy: Word and Presence
by Ian Cairns

Proverbs and Ecclesiastes: Who Knows What Is Good?
by Kathleen A. Farmer

Jeremiah 26-52: To Build, To Plant
by Walter Brueggemann

Ezekiel: A New Heart
by Bruce Vawter and Leslie J. Hoppe

NATIONS UNDER GOD

A Commentary on the Book of

1 Kings

GENE RICE

WM. B. EERDMANS PUBLISHING CO., GRAND RAPIDS

THE HANDSEL PRESS LTD, EDINBURGH

Copyright © 1990 by Wm. B. Eerdmans Publishing Co.
First published 1990 by William B. Eerdmans Publishing Company,
255 Jefferson Ave. S.E., Grand Rapids, Mich. 49503
and
The Handsel Press Limited
33 Montgomery Street, Edinburgh EH7 5JX

Library of Congress Cataloging-in-Publication Data

Rice, Gene, 1925-
Nations under God: a commentary on the book of 1 Kings / Gene Rice.
p.   cm.   —(International theological commentary)
Includes bibliographical references.
ISBN 0-8028-0492-6 (pbk.)
1. Bible. O.T. Kings, 1st—Commentaries.   I. Bible. O.T. Kings, 1st. English.
Revised Standard. 1990.   II. Title.   III. Series.
BS1335.3.R53   1990
222'.5307—dc20   90-40829
                          CIP

British Library Cataloguing in Publication Data

Rice, Gene
Nations under God
1. Bible. O.T. Kings—Critical studies
I. Title   II. Series
222.5307

ISBN 1-871828-06-6

For Betty, my wife

CONTENTS

ABBREVIATIONS

ANEP	*The Ancient Near East in Pictures,* ed. James B. Pritchard
ANET	*Ancient Near Eastern Texts,* ed. James B. Pritchard
Ant.	Josephus *Antiquities of the Jews*
JB	Jerusalem Bible
JV	Jewish Version (Jewish Publication Society Version, 1917)
KJV	King James (or Authorized) Version
LXX	Septuagint
mg	margin
Moffatt	James Moffatt, *A New Translation of the Bible*
MT	Masoretic Text
NAB	New American Bible
NASB	New American Standard Bible
NEB	New English Bible
NIV	New International Version
NJV	New Jewish Version (Jewish Publication Society, 1985)
RSV	Revised Standard Version
TEV	Today's English Version

EDITORS' PREFACE

The Old Testament alive in the Church: this is the goal of the *International Theological Commentary*. Arising out of changing, unsettled times, this Scripture speaks with an authentic voice to our own troubled world. It witnesses to God's ongoing purpose and to his caring presence in the universe without ignoring those experiences of life that cause one to question God's existence and love. This commentary series is written by front-rank scholars who treasure the life of faith.

Addressed to ministers and Christian educators, the *International Theological Commentary* moves beyond the usual critical-historical approach to the Bible and offers a *theological* interpretation of the Hebrew text. Thus, engaging larger textual units of the biblical writings, the authors of these volumes assist the reader in the appreciation of the theology underlying the text as well as its place in the thought of the Hebrew Scriptures. But more, since the Bible is the book of the believing community, its text has acquired ever more meaning through an ongoing interpretation. This growth of interpretation may be found both within the Bible itself and in the continuing scholarship of the Church.

Contributors to the *International Theological Commentary* are Christians—persons who affirm the witness of the New Testament concerning Jesus Christ. For Christians, the Bible is *one* scripture containing the Old and New Testaments. For this reason, a commentary on the Old Testament may not ignore the second part of the canon, namely, the New Testament.

Since its beginning, the Church has recognized a special relationship between the two Testaments. But the precise character of this bond has been difficult to define. Thousands of books and articles have discussed the issue. The diversity of views represented in these publications makes us aware that the Church is not of one mind in expressing the "how" of this relationship. The authors of this commentary share a developing consensus that any serious explanation of the Old Testament's relationship to the New will uphold the integrity of the Old Testament. Even though Christianity is rooted in the soil of the Hebrew Scriptures, the biblical interpreter must take care lest he or she "christianize" these Scriptures.

Authors writing in this commentary will, no doubt, hold varied views concerning *how* the Old Testament relates to the New. No attempt has been made to dictate one viewpoint in this matter. With the whole Church, we are convinced that the relationship between the two Testaments is real and substantial. But we recognize also the diversity of opinions among Christian scholars when they attempt to articulate fully the nature of this relationship.

In addition to the Christian Church, there exists another people for whom the Old Testament is important, namely, the Jewish community. Both Jews and Christians claim the Hebrew Bible as Scripture. Jews believe that the basic teachings of this Scripture point toward, and are developed by, the Talmud, which assumed its present form about 500 C.E. On the other hand, Christians hold that the Old Testament finds its fulfillment in the New Testament. The Hebrew Bible, therefore, belongs to both the Church and the Synagogue.

Recent studies have demonstrated how profoundly early Christianity reflects a Jewish character. This fact is not surprising because the Christian movement arose out of the context of first-century Judaism. Further, Jesus himself was Jewish, as were the first Christians. It is to be expected, therefore, that Jewish and Christian interpretations of the Hebrew Bible will reveal similarities *and* disparities. Such is the case. The authors of the *International Theological Commentary* will refer to the various Jewish traditions that they consider important for an appreciation of the Old Testament text. Such references will enrich our understanding of certain biblical passages and, as an extra gift, offer us insight into the relationship of Judaism to early Christianity.

An important second aspect of the present series is its *international* character. In the past, Western church leaders were considered to be *the* leaders of the Church—at least by those living in the West! The theology and biblical exegesis done by these scholars dominated the thinking of the Church. Most commentaries were produced in the Western world and reflected the life-style, needs, and thoughts of its civilization. But the Christian Church is a worldwide community. People who belong to this universal Church reflect differing thoughts, needs, and life-styles.

Today the fastest growing churches in the world are to be found, not in the West, but in Africa, Indonesia, South America, Korea, Taiwan, and elsewhere. By the end of this century, Christians in these areas will outnumber those who live in the West. In our age, especially, a commentary on the Bible must transcend the parochialism of Western civilization and be sensitive to issues that are the special problems of persons who live outside the "Christian" West, issues such as race relations, personal survival and fulfillment, liberation, revolution, famine, tyranny, disease, war, the poor, religion and state. Inspired of God, the authors of the Old Testament knew what life is like on the edge of existence. They addressed themselves to everyday people who often faced more than everyday problems. Refusing to limit God to the "spiritual," they portrayed him as one who heard and knew the cries of people in pain (see Exod. 3:7-8). The contributors to the *International Theological Commentary* are persons who prize the writings of these biblical authors as a word of life to our world today. They read the Hebrew Scriptures in the twin contexts of ancient Israel and our modern day.

The scholars selected as contributors underscore the international aspect of the series. Representing very different geographical, ideological, and ecclesiastical backgrounds, they come from more than seventeen countries. Besides scholars from such traditional countries as England, Scotland, France, Italy, Switzerland, Canada, New Zealand, Australia, South Africa, and the United States, contributors from the following places are included: Israel, Indonesia, India, Thailand, Singapore, Taiwan, and countries of Eastern Europe. Such diversity makes for richness of thought. Christian scholars living in Buddhist, Muslim, or Socialist lands may be able to offer the World Church insights into the biblical message—insights to which the scholarship of the West could be blind.

The proclamation of the biblical message is the focal concern of the *International Theological Commentary*. Generally speaking, the authors of these commentaries value the historical-critical studies of past scholars, but they are convinced that these studies by themselves are not enough. The Bible is more than an object of critical study; it is the revelation of God. In the written Word, God has disclosed himself and his will to humankind. Our authors see themselves as servants of the Word which, when rightly received, brings *shalom* to both the individual and the community.

—GEORGE A. F. KNIGHT
— FREDRICK CARLSON HOLMGREN

AUTHOR'S PREFACE

This commentary grows out of a series of classes in exegetical preaching from 1 and 2 Kings, team-taught with my colleague, Dr. Evans Crawford, professor of homiletics at the Howard University School of Divinity and dean of the University chapel. Characteristically, students began the course apprehensively. How could one preach from a book dealing with the history of the Israelite monarchy? One of the chief joys of the class was the delighted surprise of students to discover what rich resources for preaching and teaching are to be found in Kings. Many were the times when "our hearts burned within us" under the power of the proclaimed Word. The experience of working with Dean Crawford and the students in these classes greatly instructed me, and the commentary owes much to them.

I am deeply indebted to Dr. Lawrence N. Jones, dean of the Howard University School of Divinity. Without his encouragement, support—and patience—this commentary would not have been possible. A research grant from Howard University for the summers of 1987 and 1988 and a research leave granted by the Howard University School of Divinity for the spring semester of 1988 were a godsend.

I wish to express appreciation to Delores De Legall and Gloria Jackson, my research assistants, and to Jay Worrall, a good friend and neighbor. Their many valuable suggestions and careful reading of the commentary in various drafts corrected, clarified, and enriched it in many ways.

I wish also to thank Jane Hilary Rice, my daughter, for her constant encouragement and Jonathan Gregory Rice, my son, for taking time from his graduate studies at the University of Virginia to help see the manuscript into its final form. Most of all, I am thankful to my wife, Betty, for her steadfast support and the joy of her companionship in life, and it is to her that this book is fondly dedicated.

—GENE RICE

INTRODUCTION

First Kings is the story of Israel wrestling with the myriad problems of political existence from the last days of David (ca. 970 B.C.) to the beginning of the reign of Ahaziah (850). The story is unique in two respects. It is part of the first comprehensive history of a people from the ancient world. The Israelites were the first in antiquity to produce works of history as a series of meaningful events that articulate self-consciousness of identity and destiny. The historical work of which 1 Kings is a part covers the period from the time of Moses (ca. 1250) to the middle of the Babylonian Exile (561). It is a unified composition of which the following biblical books are "chapters": Deuteronomy, Joshua, Judges, 1 and 2 Samuel, 1 and 2 Kings. Because of the dominant theological influence of Deuteronomy, it is called the Deuteronomistic history.

Israel's political experience is unique, in the second place, because of the profound sense in which the state was understood to be under God. Whereas other peoples of the biblical world thought of nature as the primary theater of the divine, Israel found God to be present and involved in the arena of history and political life. The primal experience of Israel as a people was the liberation from Egyptian bondage. Through this experience the veil before life's meaning was rent in two and Israel came to know the living God who cares and liberates. That all people might share this revelation, God invited those liberated slaves to enter into covenant and charged them to be a "kingdom of priests and a holy nation" (Exod. 19:3-6), the instrument of divine blessing to all the families of the earth (Gen. 12:1-3). As God's exemplary people, Israel was held accountable especially for its conduct in the realm of political existence. Indeed, the true evidence of

1

spirituality in the Bible is to be found in social and political behavior (cf., e.g., Amos 5:21-24; Mic. 6:8; Matt. 25:31-46).

As a state Israel had to deal with taxation, the use of the nation's resources, building projects, the military, diplomacy, struggles for power, bloody revolution, civil war, and foreign invasion. These and other related problems are the subject matter of 1 Kings. The book also is concerned with building and dedicating a temple, the nature of God's presence, the power of wisdom and the power of the word of God, sin and judgment, prayer and repentance, priests and prophets, religious reform, and the administration of justice, for in ancient Israel politics and religion were inseparably related.

The major problem with which Israel struggled throughout its history, according to the Deuteronomistic history, was syncretism. Repeatedly and in the strongest terms, it is affirmed that the infiltration of the practices and values of other religions, especially Canaanite religion, is a fatal threat to Israel's integrity as God's covenant people and to its political existence. Acceptance of other gods is a violation of the First and Second Commandments, and nowhere else in the Bible is the keeping of these commandments regarded as so vital to the well-being of a people. The concern with syncretism is not speculative or theoretical. The Deuteronomistic history establishes a direct cause-and-effect relationship between the acceptance of pagan ways and values and the actual political fortunes of Israel.

The Deuteronomistic history is a genuine work of historiography that uses a variety of reliable sources, but it is not detached, descriptive history for its own sake. Rather, it is history interpreted from a theocentric perspective and written with passion and purpose. It recounts the past in order to show how Israel's history has been determined by morality, to warn of the danger of a divided heart, to summon to obedience to the commandments, to call for repentance and reform, and to prepare a people to cope with defeat and exile. It is out of these concerns that 1 Kings speaks to the present.

First Kings prods us to identify the equivalent of Canaanite religion in our own society, to consider how far antibiblical practices and values have penetrated the life of the Church and the nation, and to examine ourselves as to how seriously we take the commandments, particularly the First and Second. First Kings is especially concerned with those who limp with two different opinions (1 Kgs. 18:21) and urges them to make a commitment to follow God wholeheartedly. This concern is reinforced by sobering reminders of the tragedy that attends those who persist in following "Baal." Most of all, 1 Kings directs us to look for God's presence in the arena of public life and service, and invites us to use Israel's experience in dealing with political issues as a mirror in which to see and evaluate our own efforts. The basic affirmation of 1 Kings is that not only Israel but all nations are under God. Israel's experience gives cause to us all to ponder carefully what this means.

As a work of literature, the Deuteronomistic history is somewhat like a great cathedral built over several centuries and incorporating different architectural styles. The expert can identify the different styles and trace the stages of the cathedral's growth. Nevertheless, it is to the cathedral as a finished work that one must relate. The Deuteronomistic history exhibits both literary unity and diversity. Scholarly efforts to account for this have yielded not a consensus but three major alternative explanations: (1) the work went through two editions—the first, to support the reform of King Josiah (622-609), and the second, to deal with the fall of the nation in 587; (2) a preexilic historical work was edited periodically by a Deuteronomic school and supplemented with prophetic, priestly, and legal material; (3) it is the work of a single author utilizing many different sources whose concern was to account theologically for the fall of the nation. (For detailed expositions and critiques of these positions, see the works on the Deuteronomistic history listed in the Bibliography.)

By whatever literary process the Deuteronomistic history is to be explained, there is design and purpose in the text as it now stands, and it is this form of the text that must be interpreted. In keeping with the emphasis of the International Theological Commentary series, the writer's intention is to comprehend the text of 1 Kings both in its literal meaning and as the word of God, both as it was addressed to its original audience and as it speaks to us today.

A word of explanation is due about the usage of the term "Israel." Israel is used to designate the twelve tribes in their unity and identity as the covenant people of God, and also to refer to the kingdom formed by the ten northern tribes after the death of Solomon. To complicate matters further, Israel may designate the united kingdom of David and Solomon or the separate kingdom of Judah! Often the context is the only guide as to which sense is meant.

The writer follows the usage of the RSV in using "LORD" to designate the covenant God of Israel, Yahweh.

PART I
THE REIGN OF SOLOMON

1 Kings 1:1–11:43

HOW SOLOMON
BECAME KING
1 Kings 1:1–2:46

As part of the Deuteronomistic history, 1 Kings opens with a story already in progress. The first two chapters form the climax and conclusion to one of the most clearly defined and distinctive sources of the Deuteronomistic history, the Succession Narrative (2 Sam. 9–20; 1 Kgs. 1–2). The unity of this source has been disrupted and 2 Sam. 9–20 given a new orientation by the insertion of 2 Sam. 21–24. As a result 1 Kgs. 1–2 has been drawn into the story of Solomon and serves as the introduction to his reign.

The subject matter of 2 Sam. 9–20; 1 Kgs. 1–2 is the struggle for the succession to the throne of David and the disruption it caused in David's kingdom. The reason for the rivalry among David's sons to be king was that the constitutional procedure for determining succession had not been established. David had become king on the authority of the prophet Samuel and had displaced Israel's first king, Saul. Were prophets still to determine who would be king, or was succession to be dynastic and in order of birth? David's sons assumed that the kingship was theirs by right of birth. But David himself took no action to settle the question of succession and drifted into old age leaving the matter a troubling, anxious concern for his sons and the members of his court. This is the background of the action that unfolds in ch. 1.

HOW SOLOMON BECAME DAVID'S SUCCESSOR (1:1–53)

This chapter narrates an unexpected and dramatic development in the life of David, culminating in a day of intense action in which the smoldering issue of succession flared into a life-or-death struggle out of which Solomon emerged as David's successor. It takes up the story of life at David's court some years after the revolt of Absalom and Sheba (2 Sam. 15–20). The passage of time is vividly documented by David's physical condition. The robust, virile man who desired Bathsheba and fled on foot from Absalom is now feeble and impotent. According to 2 Sam. 5:4-5 and 1 Kgs. 2:11, David would have been seventy years old.

David's Feebleness (1:1-4)

These verses set forth the situation that forms the background to the dramatic action of the rest of the chapter. Now that he had become old, David, apparently suffering from arteriosclerosis, was unable to get warm. But more was at stake than David's health and personal well-being. This was a crisis of state.

In the biblical world the king was regarded as the link between the divine and human realms and as the channel of blessing and welfare for his people (2 Sam. 21:15-17; 23:2-4; Ps. 72; Lam. 4:20). David's vitality was therefore essential to his rule. It was for this reason that those attending David resorted to the medical remedy of securing a beautiful young maiden to rejuvenate David's vital powers by the stimulus and contagion of her youth and beauty. The text does not mention Abishag's legal status, but it is clear from 1 Kgs. 2:13-25 that she was either a wife or concubine of David.

As the serious illness of a modern head of state places his or her authority in question, so David's failure to "know" (sexually) Abishag brought on a national emergency. The purpose of this candid snapshot, painfully exposing David's feebleness, is to show that he was no longer able to function as king. The choice of a successor had become critical.

Adonijah's Bid to Become King (1:5-10)

The crisis of state occasioned by David's feebleness impelled Adonijah, David's oldest surviving son, to claim the kingship on his own initiative. David's first son, Amnon, had raped his half-sister Tamar and was killed in revenge by Tamar's full brother, Absalom (2 Sam. 13). Chileab, David's second son (2 Sam. 3:3), apparently died in childhood. Impatient for power, David's third son, Absalom, attempted to seize the throne by force, plunged the nation into civil war, and lost his life in the gamble (2 Sam. 15–18). This left Adonijah as the oldest son in order of birth. Born while David ruled in Hebron (2 Sam. 3:2-4), Adonijah would have been about forty years old.

Adonijah made public his claim to be heir-apparent by going about in a chariot with a military escort (1 Kgs. 1:5; cf. 2 Sam. 15:1). Adonijah's strategy was to win popular approval and the support of the military and religious leaders. The importance of military and religious backing would have been impressed on Adonijah by the experience of Absalom, who relied on popular support alone and lost. Adonijah sought and won the support of Joab, David's nephew (1 Chr. 2:16) and commander of Israel's volunteer army, and Abiathar, the faithful companion of David from the time of his persecution by Saul (1 Sam. 22:20-23) and high priest along with Zadok (2 Sam. 8:17). Adonijah also won wide popular support (1 Kgs. 2:15), the backing of all the Judahite royal officials, and the allegiance of all his brothers except Solomon (1:8).

Adonijah brought his campaign to a climax with a ceremonial meal at En-rogel (now called Job's Well), a spring in the Kidron Valley to the south but within earshot of Jerusalem. The text does not state the precise nature of the convocation at En-rogel, but the context implies and Nathan asserts that it was a coronation ceremony (vv. 11, 13, 24-25). A meal on such an occasion would have had a sacramental character, integrating Adonijah's followers and sealing their commitment to his cause. Absalom had also used a meal to bind his followers to him when he revolted (2 Sam. 15:11). The choice of a site for the coronation not at the nearer Gihon Spring but beyond the city limits of Jerusalem suggests a clandestine meeting.

The narrator is not without sympathy for Adonijah. He acknowledges Adonijah's claim as the oldest surviving son and appreciates Adonijah's asset of being, like Absalom, a very handsome man (1 Kgs. 1:6; cf. 1 Sam. 9:2; 16:12; 2 Sam. 14:25). Nevertheless, the narrator's disapproval is unmistakable. Adonijah "kept exalting himself, saying, 'I will be king'" (1 Kgs. 1:5 author's translation; "exalt" is a participle expressing ongoing action, and the "I" is emphatic in the Hebrew). It is a spoiled and petulant son who would be "displeased" by his father's asking, "Why have you done thus and so?" (v. 6). Also, it is an arrogant and disdainful son who aspires to be his father's successor but does not seek his father's approval and blessing. By limiting his guests to his supporters, Adonijah discloses that he was not willing to be united with his opponents in the coronation meal nor to give the people in general a voice in approving or disapproving his kingship. And through allusions to parallels with Absalom, the narrator places Adonijah in the company of his rebellious brother.

David, who was decisive as king but indulgent as a father (2 Sam. 13:21; 18:5; 19:1-8), did not interfere with Adonijah. However, there was deep division within the royal court. This division is revealed by the refusal of certain members of the cabinet and court to support Adonijah and by Adonijah's exclusion of them from his coronation (1 Kgs. 1:8, 10). Those opposed to Adonijah were Zadok the priest; Nathan the prophet; the royal bodyguard and its commander, Benaiah; Shimei and Rei (possibly officers of the bodyguard); and the non-Judahite royal officials. This group's choice for David's successor was Solomon, David's tenth son in order of birth, who would have been about twenty years old.

It is unlikely that the division within David's court was merely the result of the personal rivalry of Adonijah and Solomon. Sectional and ideological differences were undoubtedly at work polarizing the court into two parties. It is clear that a party was behind Solomon, for it is his supporters who take the lead throughout in opposing Adonijah while Solomon remains passive.

The two parties at David's court probably reflect the tension between those who were from Judah and who had followed David from the beginning and those who came into his service later and were of diverse origins. Adonijah was born in Hebron, Joab and Abiathar had been with David from the period of his fleeing from Saul, and the royal officials present at Adonijah's coronation are specifically identified as from Judah (v. 9). Solomon, on the other hand, was born in Jerusalem (2 Sam. 5:14), and Zadok, Nathan, and Benaiah are first mentioned after David became ruler over all Israel (2 Sam. 8:15-18). Adonijah's party then may have been conservative and Judahistic in orientation, while the party in support of Solomon may have been more liberal and cosmopolitan in outlook.

The issue comes down to this: at this delicate, formative juncture in history, would the destiny of Israel have been better served had Adonijah succeeded David? There was one who felt strongly that it would not. He was Nathan the prophet.

Nathan's Efforts on Behalf of Solomon (1:11-27)

While Adonijah and his company celebrate leisurely at En-rogel, Nathan makes a daring effort to annul Adonijah's kingship and to install Solomon as David's successor. This complicates Adonijah's plans and creates dramatic suspense as to the outcome. The action is now concentrated in a single day of decision and destiny that the narrator unfolds through scene and dialogue so vivid that they spontaneously stage themselves in one's imagination.

1:11-14 *Nathan's Plan.* In the first scene, an urgent Nathan calls on Bathsheba, the mother of Solomon, at the royal palace. Although not invited to the ceremony at En-rogel, Nathan was well informed about it. With the same brilliance and fearlessness with which he had called David to account because of his affair with Bathsheba, Nathan acts to foil Adonijah's plans. To implement his plan, Nathan turns to Bathsheba, the one with most immediate access to David. Identifying Adonijah as the son of David and Haggith, Nathan alludes no doubt to the rivalry between the two women, thereby galvanizing Bathsheba into action. He impresses Bathsheba with the gravity of the situation, warning her that she and Solomon are in mortal danger with Adonijah as king (1 Kgs. 1:12). Nathan's plan is for Bathsheba to remind David, by way of a question, that he had "assuredly" (KJV; emphatic *ki*) promised her on oath that Solomon would be his successor and to ask why Adonijah had become king (v. 13). To reinforce by repetition, Nathan will confirm what Bathsheba says (v. 14). Nathan is clearly the leader of the party in support of Solomon.

1:15-21 *Bathsheba's Appeal to David.* In carrying out her role, Bathsheba emerges as a forceful person with a mind of her own. Instead of asking David if he had not sworn to her that Solomon would be his successor, Bathsheba affirms that he had indeed

11

sworn that "assuredly [KJV; emphatic *ki*] Solomon your son shall reign after me" (v. 17). She declares that Adonijah has secretly made himself king, in effect charging him with treason. Bathsheba helps David comprehend what has happened by describing the ceremony at En-rogel and by identifying those invited (and who were therefore disloyal). She mentions only Solomon as excluded, thereby avoiding associating herself with Nathan, Zadok, and Benaiah. Boldly going beyond Nathan's instructions, Bathsheba assures the silent, befuddled David (Abishag's presence, v. 15, is a reminder of how feeble David was) that it was his right to determine who would succeed him and that the time for a public declaration was at hand: "And now, my lord the king, the eyes of all Israel are upon you, to tell them who shall sit on the throne of my lord the king after him" (v. 20). Bathsheba concludes with a powerful appeal to David's sympathy, declaring that after his death she and Solomon will be regarded as "traitors" (TEV, NJV).

1:22-27 *Nathan's Appeal to David.* In contrast to the impassioned Bathsheba, Nathan is courteous and dispassionate. He seeks to move David through skillfully formulated questions and insinuation. With a statement that is made into a puzzled question by the inflection of his voice, Nathan asks, "My lord the king, have you said, 'Adonijah shall reign after me, and he shall sit on my throne'?" (v. 24). Whereas Bathsheba had implied that Adonijah acted in defiance of David's will, Nathan assumes the position that Adonijah could have become king only with David's consent. Knowing that David had not authorized Adonijah's succession, Nathan both questions Adonijah's kingship and reinforces the idea that David's will was authoritative in determining his successor. Nathan also describes the gathering at En-rogel, impressing on David that it was a coronation ceremony. Adonijah's guests were "eating and drinking before him, and saying, 'Long live King Adonijah!'" (v. 25). Nathan identifies the full list of those excluded—himself, Zadok, Benaiah, and Solomon—and emphasizes that he and Solomon in particular are David's (loyal) "servants" (v. 26). Finally, Nathan asks with incredulity and wounded pride how David could have given his consent to Adonijah without informing him, his (loyal) "servant" (v. 27; reading the singular with the Qere of MT, LXX; cf. KJV, NASB), insinuating that David had betrayed the trust of his closest associate.

Solomon Is Made King (1:28-40)

Nathan's audience with David prevented the king from answering Bathsheba. Nor does David respond directly to Nathan. The story has reached its maximum moment of suspense. The climax comes when the senile, somnolent king, suddenly energized, clear of mind, and decisive, summons Bathsheba, espouses his alleged oath, and vows to execute it "today" (vv. 28-30). David also accepts Nathan's identification of those who were loyal to him. His bedroom turned into a command post, David gives crisp, precise instructions to Nathan, Zadok, and Benaiah for the coronation of Solomon (vv. 32-37). These are carried out with dispatch (vv. 38-40). David celebrates his triumph over his indecisiveness, declaring, "for he [Solomon] shall be king in my stead; and I have appointed him to be ruler over Israel and over Judah" (v. 35). Such was the power of the appeal of Nathan and Bathsheba.

1:28-30 *David's Oath.* David emphatically embraces and reiterates his alleged oath to Bathsheba that Solomon was to be his successor. The twofold characterization of the LORD, whom David invokes as witness to his oath, is a revealing statement of David's faith. He knows the LORD as the One who "lives" and as the liberating God "who has redeemed my soul out of every adversity" (v. 29; cf. 2 Sam. 4:9). Picking up on the emphatic note in Bathsheba's statement of the oath (1 Kgs. 1:17), David confirms, "*Assuredly* [emphatic *ki*] as I swore to you by the LORD, the God of Israel, saying, '*Assuredly* Solomon your son shall reign after me, and he shall sit upon my throne in my stead'; *assuredly* so I will do this day" (v. 30 author's translation). Bathsheba responds with the wish that David may "live for ever" (v. 31), that is, in the life of his descendants now that the succession is established.

1:32-40 *Solomon's Coronation.* There are three different treatments of Solomon's coronation, each supplementing the others: David's instructions (vv. 32-36), the account of their execution (vv. 38-40), and Jonathan's report to Adonijah at En-rogel (vv. 43-48).

13

The first act of the coronation ceremony was a procession to the Gihon Spring located on the west slope of the Kidron Valley beneath the walled city of Jerusalem (presently called "Spring of the Mother of Steps" by Arabs and "Spring of the Virgin" by Christians). The procession included Zadok, Nathan, Benaiah, David's royal officials who had not supported Adonijah, and the royal bodyguard of Cherethites and Pelethites (i.e., Cretans and Philistines). The urgency of the situation did not allow for the participation of the general public.

Solomon rode on David's mule, tangible proof that he was David's choice. Only recently introduced into Israel, the mule was a symbol of royal authority and privilege (2 Sam. 13:29; 18:9). The common animal for riding was the ass (2 Sam. 17:23; 1 Kgs. 2:40); horses at this time were used only for chariots. The rarity and special status of the mule, which was imported (10:25; Ezek. 27:14), was due no doubt to the prohibitions of cross-breeding (Lev. 19:19).

At Gihon Solomon was anointed, the trumpet was blown, and all exclaimed, "Long live King Solomon!" Anointing was an act of consecration, authorization, and empowerment. It brought the king into the relationship of sonship to God (Ps. 2:7) and made his person sacrosanct (1 Sam. 24:6, 10; 26:9, 11, 23; 2 Sam. 1:14-16). By virtue of his office, the king was the recipient of God's "steadfast, sure love" (Isa. 55:3). As ruler he was the maintainer of justice, righteousness, and peace, the channel of blessing and well-being for his people, and God's viceroy and witness to the nations (2 Sam. 23:2-4; Ps. 72; Isa. 55:3-5). Both Zadok and Nathan participated in the rite of anointing, but their respective roles are not defined (1 Kgs. 1:34, 39, 45). Possibly Nathan delivered an oracle articulating the nature of the office of the king (cf. Ps. 110) and Zadok administered the anointing oil (1 Kgs. 1:39). There is no mention of the anointing of Adonijah.

The acclamation "Long live King Solomon!" (cf. 1 Sam. 10:24; 2 Sam. 16:16; 1 Kgs. 1:25; 2 Kgs. 11:12) expresses both the consent of the people and the wish for divine vitality to be concentrated in the person of the king so that he in turn may enhance their lives.

From Gihon Solomon returned to the city, and "all the people went up after him, playing on pipes, and rejoicing with great joy, so that the earth was split by their noise" (1 Kgs. 1:40) and the city was "in an uproar" (v. 45). Then Solomon took his seat on the royal throne to receive the homage of his subjects. The final scene of the coronation takes place in David's bedroom, where David's chief officials come to congratulate him. They express the wish that God will make Solomon's "name" (fame, renown) and "throne" (rule) even greater than David's (v. 47; cf. vv. 36-37), foreshadowing the glory of Solomon's reign. David responds by blessing (i.e., giving honor to) the LORD for granting "one of my offspring to sit on my throne this day" (v. 48). The narrator wants us to understand that Solomon's accession was the fulfillment of Nathan's prophecy (2 Sam. 7:12).

Two terms are used for the royal office: "king" (1 Kgs. 1:34, 35a) and "ruler" (v. 35b). "King" *(melek)* had a long history of usage and carried with it associations of autocracy and despotism from the practice of kingship among Israel's neighbors. "Ruler" *(nagid,* translated elsewhere as "prince" or "leader"), a term unique to Israelite tradition, emphasizes that one rules at God's appointment and pleasure (cf. 1 Sam. 9:16; 10:1; 13:14; 25:30; 2 Sam. 7:8; 1 Kgs. 14:7; 16:2). These two terms anticipate the long struggle between the ideal and the practice of kingship in Israel.

The Collapse of Adonijah's Bid to Be King (1:41-53)

David's oath and instructions for Solomon's coronation settle the struggle for the succession in Solomon's favor and annul Adonijah's kingship. Thus the day of decision ends at En-rogel, as it began there, but in a complete reversal of the positions of Adonijah and Solomon. Within a matter of minutes the mood of Adonijah and his guests swings from festive celebration to apprehension aroused by the noise in the city (1 Kgs. 1:41) to reassurance when Jonathan arrives (v. 42) to trembling and flight when they hear Jonathan's report (vv. 43-49). To Adonijah's wishful hope that Jonathan brings good news, Jonathan replies, "I'm afraid not" (TEV), and he heaps up the bad news with a threefold "moreover" (vv. 46, 47, 48, smoothed out in the RSV). It was David's authority, pointedly accepted by Jonathan, that settled the matter. "Our lord King David," Jonathan says, "has made Solomon king" (v. 43; cf. v. 47). David's decision is sealed by the endorsement of the chief royal officials (v. 47; cf. vv. 36-37) and by David's thanksgiving to God for Solomon's accession (v. 48). Solomon also had the advantage of the presence and support of the royal bodyguard.

By seeking refuge at the altar (vv. 50-51), although not threatened by Solomon, Adonijah betrays a guilty conscience and confirms Nathan's warning that Adonijah as king would have dealt violently with Solomon and Bathsheba (v. 12). Solomon makes Adonijah responsible for his own fate. If he proves to be a "worthy man"—that is, if his behavior corresponds to that which is appropriate to one of royal status—he has nothing to fear, but "wickedness" will cost him his life (vv. 52-53).

THEOLOGICAL REFLECTIONS ON CHAPTER 1

This chapter deals with the problem of selecting a leader under very complex and ambiguous circumstances. The choice was a critical one. Although David had united Israel and ruled a small empire, the foundations of an enduring kingdom had yet to be established. The religious institutions of the tribal confederacy had not been adapted nor a theology formulated to prepare Israel to serve God in its new imperial status. Adonijah's character and the way he sought the kingship (and his foolish request for Abishag, 2:13-25) suggest that he would have placed the kingdom on a very shaky foundation. Clearly, Adonijah would have been David's successor and the history of Israel would have taken a different course, had it not been for the intervention of Nathan.

Nathan was a prophet, and it was the prerogative of a prophet in those days to determine who would be king. The prophet could both designate one to be king and dismiss him from office, as Samuel had Saul. Also, Nathan had mediated God's covenant to David and his dynasty (2 Sam. 7), and as the mediator of this covenant he would have been concerned that the dynasty be shaped by the best and ablest of David's sons. According to 2 Sam. 12:24-25, it had been revealed to Nathan from the beginning that Solomon was especially loved by the LORD. It is with good reason that Nathan is consistently referred to in 1 Kgs. 1 and 2 as "the prophet." In intervening on behalf of Solomon, Nathan acted in his office as prophet.

Divine authorization of Nathan's intervention is confirmed by the responses to it. It is as if David were waiting to be reminded that he had taken an oath that Solomon would be his successor, and he gladly acknowledges and affirms it (1:29-30). David felt God's presence through the appeal of Nathan and Bathsheba and regards it as another instance of God's liberating him out of adversity (v. 29). The ultimate confirmation comes from David's thanksgiving to God for granting "one of my offspring to sit on my throne this day" (v. 48). This statement means that the seal of divine approval rests solidly on Solomon's kingship (and that the divine purpose was achieved by Nathan's intervention). Secondary confirmation is given by Benaiah's "Amen," an official formula of assent (Num. 5:22; Deut. 27:15-26), and his good wishes for Solomon (1 Kgs. 1:36-37, 47). Even the enthusiasm of the crowd for Solomon (vv. 40, 45) bespeaks the divine approval of Nathan's actions.

The major theological point of ch.1 is that God was present in the complex and ambiguous circumstances surrounding the succession of Solomon. Indeed, in spite of these circumstances, God's will was realized. This passage is no brief for withdrawal from hard choices, nor does it countenance letting the complexity and ambiguity of a situation paralyze one into inaction. The chapter is a summons to the man or woman of God to be in the midst of the rowdy, untidy push and shove of human striving where God's purposes are at stake and to act with the boldness and astuteness of a Nathan. Bad leadership and evil can succeed only with the consent of the righteous. "I told you so" is no substitute for responsible action.

In fulfilling his role as prophet, Nathan did not passively wait for God to work a miracle. Instead, boldly, aggressively, and with keen psychological insight he exploited the situation to achieve his purpose. The children of this world tend to be more committed to their cause and more astute in dealing with their affairs than the children of light (Luke 16:8). Astuteness and right conduct are not contradictory terms. If the righteousness of the followers of Jesus should exceed that of the scribes and Pharisees (Matt. 5:20), should not the astuteness of the children of light exceed that of the children of darkness? There is a risk, of course—a risk of acting without adequate knowledge or in defense of prejudice or in support of misguided ambition. The mandate of 1 Kgs. 1 will be best served by being "wise as serpents [the most subtle of creatures, Gen. 3:1] and innocent as doves" (Matt. 10:16).

As a prophet and mediator of God's covenant with David (2 Sam. 7), Nathan would have acted out of concern for the well-being of David's dynasty and kingdom. And in fact, David's dynasty did endure for some four hundred years, a remarkable record in the turbulent politics of the biblical world. Even when deprived of political power, it lived on as an ideal and in the fullness of time yielded One far greater than David and Solomon. Who would have anticipated on that fateful day of decision that Nathan's intervention would have such a glorious outcome, that David and the "wife of Uriah," through Solomon, were to become forebears of the Messiah (Matt. 1:6)! Hard choices are often like that.

DAVID'S LAST WILL AND TESTAMENT (2:1-12)

Apparently soon after the events of 1 Kgs. 1 David died. As did Jacob (Gen. 49), Moses (Deut. 33), Joshua (Josh. 23), and Samuel (1 Sam. 12), David used the occasion of his approaching death to issue his last will and testament. What concerned David most at this time in his life was his dynasty. Here David sets forth his ideal of kingly rule in a series of admonitions (1 Kgs. 2:2-4) and then gives specific instructions to remove certain threats to his dynasty (vv. 5-9). Framing David's farewell charge to Solomon is the anticipation of his death (v. 1) and his obituary (vv. 10-12).

The Key to Successful Leadership (2:2-4)

2:2-3a *The Requirements of Good Government.* David's first admonition is to "be strong" (v. 2), a requirement basic to leadership in general. But David does not stop there. He adds the important qualification that strength is to be rooted in morality. Solomon is exhorted to walk in the ways of the LORD and to keep the LORD's statutes, commandments, ordinances, and testimonies (v. 3). The LORD's ways are not vague and mysterious but are clearly defined. "Statutes" *(huqqot)* and "commandments" *(mitswot)* are the absolute, unqualified requirements of God stated as "Thou shalt" or "Thou shalt not." "Ordinances" *(mishpatim)* are legal precedents built up by custom by which specific cases are judged. "Testimonies" *('edot)* are laws viewed as the personal attestations of God's will. These terms are used more or less synonymously (cf. Ps. 19:7-9), and all refer to "the law of Moses," which for 1-2 Kings is specifically Deuteronomy (2 Kgs. 14:6; cf. Deut. 17:18-20; 24:16).

The Hebrew word *torah,* traditionally rendered by "law," does not have the burdensome and legalistic connotation of the English term. For the Israelite *torah* was a precious gift and the source of life (Deut. 30:11-20), more to be desired than gold and sweeter than honey (Ps. 19:10; cf. Ps. 119). The best English equivalents are "instruction," "guidance," "direction."

2:3b-4 *The Rewards of Right Rule.* David gives two reasons why Solomon should heed his admonitions. By ruling according to them (1) Solomon will prosper in all he does, and (2) God will establish his "word" that if David's sons are obedient he will always have a descendant on the throne of Israel.

There is some difficulty with the identification of God's word to David. One thinks first of all of God's covenant with David in 2 Sam. 7 (esp. vv. 12-16). But there God promises David *unconditionally* that "your house [dynasty] and your kingdom shall be made sure for ever before me; your throne shall be established for ever" (2 Sam. 7:16). Moreover, in 1 Kgs. 11:36; 15:4-5; 2 Kgs. 8:19 the unconditional promise of 2 Sam. 7 is related specifically to Judah and Jerusalem. The difficulty in 1 Kgs. 2 may be due to the ambiguous nature of the term "Israel," which may refer either to all Israel (1:34) or only to the northern tribes (2 Sam. 2:9, 10; 1 Kgs. 1:35; 11:37). The monarchy of David and Solomon was actually a dual monarchy consisting of Israel *and* Judah (2 Sam. 12:8; 1 Kgs. 1:35; 2:32). David made a separate covenant with the northern tribes (2 Sam. 5:1-3), and the allusion to it in 1 Kgs. 11:11 suggests it was conditional. Furthermore, all other references to this conditional covenant (8:25; 9:4-5) have to do with Solomon, the only monarch after David to rule over all the tribes. In this context then (and in 8:25; 9:4-5) God's word to David most likely refers to the covenant with the northern tribes and the conditions of rule over them (cf. Richard D. Nelson, *The Double Redaction of the Deuteronomistic History*, 101-5).

David's Instructions concerning His Dynasty (2:5-9)

The second part of David's farewell address is on a different plane from 2:2-4 and moves within an ancient thought world. Here David charges Solomon to remove the bloodguilt on his dynasty incurred by Joab's murder of Abner and Amasa, to provide a place at his table for the sons of Barzillai, and to neutralize Shimei's curse.

2:5-6 *Instructions concerning Joab.* In Israelite thinking, blood shed unjustly demands requital (Gen. 4:10; Job 16:18). The victim's blood clings to the murderer and threatens him with an awesome power that will not be turned away until the blood of the guilty party is shed (Gen. 9:6; Num. 35:33; Judg. 9:22-25, 56-57; 2 Sam. 21:1-9). Joab shed unjustly the blood of Abner (2 Sam. 3:17-27; cf. 2:13-23) and Amasa (20:4-10); as Joab's commander-in-chief, David was responsible for Joab's actions. What Joab did, he did to David and to David's dynasty (cf. 1 Kgs. 2:33). To remove this threat to his dynasty David directs Solomon to find a way to turn the responsibility for the deaths of Abner and Amasa back on Joab upon whom it properly belonged (2 Sam. 3:28-29, 39).

2:7 *Instruction concerning Barzillai's Sons.* When Absalom revolted, David fled to Gilead where he was generously befriended by Barzillai (2 Sam. 7:27-29; cf. 19:31-40). David's directive that Solomon let Barzillai's sons be among those who ate at his table was in effect the granting of a pension. There is power in loyalty and kindness as well as in unjustly shed blood.

2:8-9 *Instructions concerning Shimei.* According to Israelite psychology a curse was "a poisonous, consuming substance that destroys and undermines" (Johannes Pedersen, *Israel, Its Life and Culture*, I-II, 437). Once uttered, a curse "was conceived as having objective existence, and endowed with self-fulfilling energy" (John

Skinner, *I and II Kings,* 72; cf. Zech. 5:1-4). Shimei had cursed David with a "grievous curse" when David fled from Absalom (1 Kgs. 2:8; cf. 2 Sam. 16:5-8). Cursing a ruler was a capital offense (Exod. 22:28), but because Shimei had apologized profusely to David after Absalom's defeat David had sworn not to take his life (2 Sam. 19:16-23). Shimei's guilt, however, remained, and as long as he lived his curse retained its power to harm David's dynasty. Because his oath to spare Shimei would cease to be effective after his death, David asks Solomon to find a way to eliminate the threat of Shimei's curse.

David's Obituary (2:10-12)

For all David's achievements and the esteem with which he was held, his obituary conforms with slight variation to a standard format. The place of burial was Jerusalem, David's personal holding ("city of David") by right of conquest (2 Sam. 5:6-9). The length of David's reign was forty years, seven in Hebron and thirty-three in Jerusalem (1 Kgs. 2:11; cf. 2 Sam. 5:4-5). His successor was his son Solomon, whose "kingdom was firmly established" (1 Kgs. 2:12). This comment anticipates v. 46 and reflects the intense interest in the problem of succession in chs. 1 and 2. In this context, the meaning must be that it was David's instructions to Solomon that made the kingdom secure.

THEOLOGICAL REFLECTIONS ON 2:1-12

The ideal of kingly rule according to David is strength rooted in morality (vv. 2-4). Weakness invites dissension, the triumph of bad leadership, and evil. But strength is not for the personal, arbitrary, or despotic use of the ruler. Above kingship—and leadership in general—stands God's *torah,* limiting and conditioning all human exercise of power. If one would be a successful ruler or leader, one must walk before God in truth *(emet)* and with all one's heart and soul (v. 4). That is, the ruler must live in steadfast, trustful dependence on God and be committed to God with one's total inner being—intellect, will, and emotions.

Given David's thought world and presuppositions, the unrequited blood of Abner and Amasa and the curse of Shimei posed serious threats to his dynasty. The revolts of Absalom and Sheba and Adonijah's bid for the kingship must have impressed David with the importance of anticipating and dealing with potential trouble. David's instructions to Solomon reveal a man determined that his dynasty would not be vulnerable in any way. His concern is a reminder that good leadership, if it is to endure, must maintain itself against whoever would weaken or overthrow it. Such a concern should be tempered by the awareness that it is a short step from firmly established authority to tyranny—and that theological reasons may be used to justify personal ambition.

SOLOMON MAKES HIS KINGSHIP SECURE (2:13-46)

Solomon is now king, but his throne is not secure. The threat of the bloodguilt incurred by Joab and the curse of Shimei lurk over him. Also, Adonijah and his supporters are free to pursue their schemes and to exploit any opportunity to advance their cause.

Having been placed under solemn obligation to remove the threats to his rule (2:5-9), Solomon patiently awaits an opportunity, and when it presents itself he acts swiftly and decisively. That opportunity comes unexpectedly. David had not reckoned with Adonijah as a source of trouble, but it is from him that Solomon first feels his rule challenged. In dealing with Adonijah, Solomon also has occasion to carry out David's instructions concerning Joab. This takes place on a single day of intense activity reminiscent of ch. 1. The removal of Shimei's curse requires another time and different circumstances.

2:13-25 *Adonijah's Request for Abishag.* On the surface this is a poignant and tragic story in which Adonijah loses his life for the love of a beautiful maiden. But is this a case of Adonijah being sincere but naive, or is his request for Abishag a sinister ploy to reassert his claim to be king? Is Bathsheba's support genuine or hypocritical? Does Solomon use Adonijah's request as a pretext to take his life, or is Solomon justified in his sentence? It is impossible to ascertain the true motives of the characters in this little drama, but the speeches of Adonijah and Solomon shed additional light on the struggle for the succession.

In asking Bathsheba to make known to Solomon his desire for

Abishag, Adonijah speaks about his claim to the kingship, and for the first time we learn how he felt about it. To Bathsheba he says, "You know that the kingdom was *mine* [emphatic in the Hebrew], and that all Israel fully expected me to reign; however, the kingdom has turned about and become my brother's, for it was his from the LORD" (2:15). This inadvertent confession, all the more significant as coming from the one displaced by Solomon, is an important interpretive key to the events of ch. 1. Along with David's blessing (1:48), it affirms that Solomon's succession was in accordance with God's will and that it was through Nathan's intervention that God turned the kingdom about.

Whatever Adonijah's intentions, his request for Abishag was fraught with risk. The women of a deceased or displaced king belonged to his successor and were symbolic of the new king's legitimacy and authority (2 Sam. 3:6-11; 12:8; 16:20-22). The effect of this request on Solomon shows how explosive it was. It transformed him from one who graciously promised to refuse his mother nothing to one who angrily rejects her request. Construing Adonijah's petition as a blatant bid for his throne, Solomon bitingly asks, "And why do you ask [only] Abishag the Shunammite for Adonijah? Ask for him the kingdom also . . ." (1 Kgs. 2:22). The offense is so flagrant that Solomon takes an oath to exact the death penalty (v. 23) and in a second oath (v. 24) vows to execute it "today."

Solomon's reaction also reveals how vulnerable he feels himself to be. He regards the fact that Adonijah is David's oldest surviving son as a powerful claim that could be used against him. And he is uneasy that Adonijah still receives the support of Abiathar and Joab.

Verses 13-25 contain the first statement from Solomon as to how he perceived his succession and kingship. In his oath to the LORD sealing his decision to take Adonijah's life he gives credit to the LORD as the one "who has established me, and placed me on the throne of David my father, and who has made me a house, as he promised" (v. 24). This is another key theological statement affirming that Solomon's kingship is the fulfillment of God's promise through Nathan to build a house (i.e., a dynasty) for David (2 Sam. 7:11). Solomon's attitude stands in contrast to that of Adonijah, who regarded the kingship as his personal possession ("the kingdom was mine," 1 Kgs. 2:15).

23

2:26-27, 35b *Abiathar's Banishment.* Additional evidence that Solomon genuinely feared treachery from Adonijah is provided by his removal of Abiathar from his priestly office. Solomon does not specify the charge against Abiathar, but from the context it can only be his perceived support of Adonijah's scheme to regain the kingship. Solomon judges Abiathar to be deserving of the death penalty—confirmation of the treasonable nature of his offense—but conditionally commutes it to exile at Abiathar's estate in Anathoth, about 5 km. (3 mi.) NE of Jerusalem. The agony this cost Abiathar is anticipated in the prophecy against Eli's priestly house in 1 Sam. 2:33: "The man of you [Eli] whom I shall not cut off from my altar [Abiathar] shall be spared to weep out his eyes and grieve his heart. . . ."

Following the dismissal of Abiathar, Solomon makes Zadok chief priest (1 Kgs. 2:35b), thereby placing his family in a position of privilege that led to its preeminence over other priestly families in the subsequent history of the priesthood. The background of Zadok is shadowy. He is first mentioned in 2 Sam. 8:17 without any indication of his previous history. Some scholars have conjectured that he was originally a priest of the native Jebusite cult of Jerusalem and became a convert to the faith of Israel after David conquered the city. According to 1 Chr. 6:3-8, 50-53; 24:3, however, Zadok was descended from Eleazar, Aaron's third and oldest surviving son after the deaths of Nadab and Abihu (Lev. 10:1-7).

Abiathar's banishment is declared to be the fulfillment of the prophecy spoken against his ancestor Eli (1 Sam. 2:27-36), the descendant of Ithamar, Aaron's youngest son (Exod. 6:23; Num. 3:2-3). By the time 1–2 Kings was completed the descendants of Zadok were regarded as the sole legitimate priests with the right to offer sacrifice (Ezek. 40:46; 44:10-14; Num. 3:10; 18:1-7). This passage, clearly partisan to the Zadokites, regards this development as providential. Eli's descendants, however, retained their status as priests (Jer. 1:1) and functioned in a minor capacity in the Second Temple (1 Chr. 24; Josephus *Ant.* viii.1, 3).

2:28-35a *Removal of Joab's Bloodguilt.* Solomon's treatment of Adonijah and Abiathar means to Joab that his life is in danger and he seeks refuge at the altar. As custodian of the sanctuary, Solomon overrules the right of refuge and has Joab executed. Apparently Joab thought his only offense was complicity with Adonijah (1 Kgs. 2:28). But Solomon also holds him culpable for the murder of Abner and Amasa, an offense not covered by the right of refuge (Exod. 21:12-14; Deut. 27:24).

Solomon's real concern is to take away from himself and his dynasty "the guilt for the blood which Joab shed without cause" (1 Kgs. 2:31). By the just retribution of Joab's death, the blood of Abner and Amasa is brought back on Joab and his family, the demand for requital is satisfied, and David's dynasty is free to become the recipient of "peace *(shalom)* from the LORD for evermore" (vv. 32-33).

In acknowledgment of Joab's devotion to David, Solomon honors him in death by permitting him to be buried at his home "in the open country" *(midbar;* TEV) at Bethlehem (v. 34; cf. 2 Sam. 2:32). Following Joab's death, Solomon appoints Benaiah commander of all the armed forces (1 Kgs. 2:35a).

2:36-46a *Removal of Shimei's Curse.* The remaining threat to David's dynasty was Shimei's curse. Shimei was not involved with Adonijah in any way, so Solomon has to deal with him separately. Without explanation, Solomon requires Shimei to leave his estate in Bahurim (v. 8), a village a short distance NE of Jerusalem, and reside in Jerusalem. Political considerations may have prompted Solomon to take this action, for Shimei was a relative of Saul (2 Sam. 16:5) and the revolt of Sheba (2 Sam. 20) was proof of the readiness of Benjaminites to break away from the house of David. Possibly Shimei had taken Sheba's place as the leader of the Benjaminites. Whatever his motives, Solomon forbids Shimei to leave Jerusalem and, in particular, to cross the brook Kidron separating Jerusalem and Bahurim, on pain of death.

Jerusalem at this time was a small city occupying an area slightly less than 11 acres. To be confined to so small a space and to be cut off from his estate, kindred, and friends must have been very trying to Shimei, but he endured it for some three years. However, when two of his slaves escaped and sought refuge in Gath, Shimei went to reclaim them. Shimei's presence may have been required to negotiate the return of his slaves, and he may have thought Solomon would not mind his going to Gath since he did not cross the brook Kidron. But Solomon had also stipulated that Shimei was not to go forth "to any place whatever" (1 Kgs. 2:36, 42).

Upon Shimei's return, Solomon confronts him, charges him with violating his oath, and asks for an explanation (vv. 41-43). Shimei has no answer, and Solomon exacts the death penalty, declaring that the LORD is at work in what transpires to bring back on Shimei's head "the evil" he did to David by his curse (v. 44). The removal of Shimei's curse opens the way for blessing upon Solomon and for the throne of David to be "established before the LORD for ever" (v. 45). Solomon sees the power of God's promise to David and his dynasty at work in the retribution on Shimei as well as on Adonijah (2 Sam. 7:13, 16, 26).

2:46b *The Establishment of the Kingdom in Solomon's Hand.* With the removal of Shimei's curse David's instructions are carried out and all threats to Solomon's rule are eliminated. The tension with which the long struggle for the succession has been charged is resolved and the narrator can say at last: "So the kingdom was established in the hand of Solomon." This statement is an affirmation that the events of 2 Sam. 9–20; 1 Kgs. 1–2 have worked together providentially for this outcome.

THEOLOGICAL REFLECTIONS ON 2:13-46

The manner in which Solomon carried out David's instructions raises the problem of the tension between power and justice. David charged Solomon to be strong but also to exercise his power in obedience to God. In his treatment of Adonijah, Abiathar, Joab, and Shimei, Solomon clearly acted in strength. But were his motives pure and his behavior moral?

These questions must be answered in terms of the psychology and legal traditions of ancient Israel. According to these, the measures Solomon took were permissible if not mandatory. Had Solomon granted Adonijah's request for Abishag, his authority would have been seriously undermined. Likewise, the bloodguilt of Joab and the curse of Shimei were perceived as a cancerous growth on David's dynasty.

Solomon acts only after his opponents have made themselves culpable by their own behavior. When Solomon pronounces sentence he is careful to establish guilt and to give the reasons for his judicial decisions. He is also sensitive to God at work in the course of events (vv. 24, 32, 44; cf. v. 27). David's failure to deal firmly with Amnon for his violation of his sister Tamar and with Absalom when he murdered Amnon led to alienation within David's family, civil war, and the loss of many lives (2 Sam. 13–18). Given the two rival parties for the succession (see above on 1 Kgs. 1:5-10) and Solomon's tenuous hold on the kingship, would not any sign of weakness by Solomon have led to similar consequences? Compared to the struggle for succession following the death of Henry VIII of England or the wholesale liquidation of the political opposition in modern totalitarian states, Solomon acted with restraint. In all, three persons lost their lives and one person was removed from office. There is no record of further bloodshed at Solomon's command during the rest of his reign. And Solomon did go on to do great things. This was made possible largely by the measures he took to strengthen his dynasty and kingdom at the outset.

There is a delicately balanced point in leadership between weakness and despotism where firmness and strength in the cause of justice and right may be exercised in submission to God and in obedience to his will. It is the task of leadership to find this vantage point and to act from it. The task is all the more urgent because of the complex and difficult problems of modern society.

1 Kgs. 2:46b serves as an interpretive key to the struggle for the succession viewed as a whole. The violent discord within David's family that breaks out in chs. 1–2 is the final expression of the nemesis of judgment on David resulting from his affair with Bathsheba. Because of David's sin, God raised up evil against David out of his own house (2 Sam. 12:11). Taken as a whole, 2 Sam. 9–20; 1 Kgs. 1–2 is one of the most powerful indictments of sin in the Bible. But this material has to do with more than judgment. Running parallel to the nemesis of judgment are the grace and providence of God. The child born of the adulterous union died, but another son was born to David and Bathsheba (2 Sam. 12:15-25). David almost lost his kingdom to Absalom, but God defeated the counsel of Ahithophel and David regained his throne (2 Sam. 16:15–17:14). The ultimate good in this tangle of events was the accession of that son of David whom the LORD

loved (2 Sam. 12:24-25), who ended the disruption in David's family and established the kingdom in strength and peace. Good and evil mingle together in these events. But God is able to achieve his purposes in the midst of and in spite of evil. Even that which is meant for evil God can turn to good (Gen. 45:8; 50:20; Ps. 76:9). The supreme example of this, of course, was the turning of Good Friday into Easter.

In contrast to other portions of the OT, in 1 Kgs. 1–2 God does not make himself known in dramatic, perceptible ways. The real locus of God's activity is the human heart. It is there, in the decisions men and women make as they deal with the demands of life, that God is present and his purposes are realized. The following chapters will emphasize the importance of purity of worship. Chapters 1–2 of 1 Kings are a powerful testimony of the individual's responsibility for the purity of the heart and the importance of what happens there.

SOLOMON'S EMPOWERMENT TO RULE

1 Kings 3:1-28

As one turns from ch. 2 to ch. 3 it is clear that a threshold has been crossed. The vivid, flowing narrative of chs. 1 and 2 gives way for the most part to reports, lists, and accounts that catalogue and enumerate factual information about Solomon's reign. Underlying the change in literary style is the use of different sources. Principal among these is "the book of the acts of Solomon," a popular work celebrating "the acts of Solomon, and all that he did, and his wisdom" (11:41). Other sources drawn upon but not named are royal annals and temple archives, stories about prophets, and a vast reservoir of popular lore.

The account of Solomon's reign is organized around four principal subjects: Solomon the administrator (ch. 4), Solomon the builder (5:1–9:25), Solomon the trader (9:26–10:29), and Solomon the sinner (ch. 11). Solomon's achievements as builder and trader are truly outstanding, and the picture of his reign in chs. 4–10 is one of splendor and glory. Never again was Israel to know such security, peace, and material well-being. The basis of Solomon's success as a ruler was an experience at Gibeon (3:4-15). The account of this experience is prefaced by three notes (3:1, 2, 3).

THE MARRIAGE ALLIANCE WITH EGYPT (3:1)

Of Solomon's many marriages, only the one to Pharaoh's daughter is singled out for mention. It dramatically confirms that "the kingdom was established in the hand of Solomon" (2:46b). What could be more striking proof that Solomon was recognized as the rightful king of Israel than marriage to an Egyptian princess? And what a reversal of Israel's fortunes this marriage represents—a descendant of those formerly enslaved by Egypt is now Pharaoh's son-in-law! This note also serves to contrast Solomon's successful suit of Pharaoh's daughter with Adonijah's foolish request for Abishag (2:13-25).

The marriage was political, "a marriage alliance with Pharaoh king of Egypt." The Pharaoh in question was most likely Siamun (978-959 B.C.) or Psusennes II (959-945) of the 21st Dynasty. Egypt was Israel's only serious rival at the time, and the alliance was an important asset to Solomon's fledgling kingdom. It made for peace, had mutual commercial benefits, and opened up to Israel the vast experience of Egypt in learning and government.

In recognition of the special nature of this marriage, Solomon built a palace for his Egyptian wife, but not "until he had finished building his own house and the house of the LORD and the wall around Jerusalem." Pharaoh's daughter had to wait twenty years for her palace (9:24). The period of her wait provides a convenient time frame for Solomon's most important building projects and indicates the priority he gave them.

WORSHIP AT THE HIGH PLACES (3:2, 3)

High places were local open air sanctuaries. Many had been taken over from the Canaanites and were open invitations to the seductive attraction of Canaanite cultic practice and ideology. The threat of Canaanite religion was not perceived at first, and the high places were regarded as acceptable places of worship by all, including Solomon. From the vantage point of the later editors of 1–2 Kings, however, it was awkward that Solomon was granted the gift of wisdom during a worship service at the high place at Gibeon (3:4-15). Verses 2 and 3 are editorial notes that explain and defend Solomon's practice of worshipping at the high places.

Verse 3 seems to have been the first effort to account for Solomon's behavior. It regards Solomon's worship at the high places as regrettable but minimizes it on the grounds that Solomon "loved the LORD" and lived according to "the statutes of David." Verse 2 would excuse Solomon altogether on the grounds that the temple had not been built and everyone worshipped at the high places.

THEOLOGICAL REFLECTIONS ON 3:1-3

Solomon is famous for his wisdom, piety, and his great contribution in building the temple, but in the end he stands under judgment for his sins. Solomon's reign was one of peace, prosperity and splendor, but it ended in strife and the division of the kingdom. Verses 1-3 imply that the seeds of the ignoble end of Solomon's reign were sown from the beginning. There was great political advantage in marrying a daughter of Pharaoh but also a risk to the integrity of Solomon's commitment to the LORD (11:1-13). 1 Kgs. 3:2, 3 illustrate the kinds of rationalizations that make sin acceptable. Verse 2 uses the argument, "Everyone is doing it." Verse 3 creates the illusion that it is possible to love God and live a moral life and still "worship at the high places." Silently, invisibly, like an incubating virus, sin was at work throughout Solomon's reign and in the end broke out in violent, destructive force. Such is the nature of sin.

SOLOMON'S DREAM AT GIBEON (3:4-15)

From this passage it is clear that all that happens in chs. 1 and 2 is preliminary. The real beginning of Solomon's reign was a spiritual experience at Gibeon that empowered him for the proper exercise of his kingship. All the achievements for which Solomon is so famous are rooted in this occasion.

3:4 *The Pilgrimage to Gibeon.* The chief sanctuary at the beginning of Solomon's reign was the high place at Gibeon, 11 km. (7 mi.) NW of Jerusalem. The high place itself is usually identified with Nebi Samwil, a prominent hill a short distance south of Gibeon. How Gibeon became "the great high place" is obscure. The Gibeonites negotiated a separate treaty with Israel at the time of the conquest (Josh. 9–10) and became worshippers of the LORD (Josh. 9:9) but retained their identity (2 Sam. 21:1-6).

It appears that in the aftermath of the fall of Shiloh (1 Sam. 4) Gibeon succeeded that city as the chief sanctuary in Israel. Apparently it was to Gibeon that the people of Kiriath-jearim brought the ark after it was captured and released by the Philistines (1 Sam. 7:1-2; 2 Sam. 6:3; 1 Chr. 16:37-39). The house of

Abinadab where they left the ark was situated "on the hill" (Gibeon in Hebrew means "little hill"). There the ark remained for twenty years until David brought it to Jerusalem. The tent of meeting/tabernacle was also located at Gibeon during the time of David and Solomon according to 1 Chr. 16:37-39; 21:29; 2 Chr. 1:3, 5, 6, 13. It was presumably the presence of these ancient, hallowed emblems that led to the high place of Gibeon being called "the mountain of the LORD" (2 Sam. 21:6).

All Israelites were obliged to gather at the central sanctuary for the celebration of Passover, Weeks or Pentecost, and Booths or Ingathering (Exod. 23:14-17). There is nothing about Solomon's pilgrimage to Gibeon, however, that points to one of these festivals. This was a special occasion.

It was a practice of monarchs of the biblical world, especially in Egypt, before some great undertaking or innovation to make a pilgrimage to a sanctuary to seek authorization and direction. This was done according to prescribed ritual, and the divine response traditionally came in a dream (*ANET,* 449). Solomon's journey to Gibeon should be understood in the light of this practice. As the context indicates, he went there seeking divine help as he prepared to assume the full responsibilities of government.

3:5 *God's Appearance and Invitation.* This verse bypasses the details of ritual preparation and goes directly to the revelatory experience. It took place at night and came in the form of a dream. The LORD appears to Solomon, but no circumstantial details are given. The narrator is interested only in the dream itself. The dream is unfolded through dialogue that God initiates by inviting Solomon to "Ask what I shall give you."

3:6-9 *Solomon's Request.* Solomon prefaces his request by acknowledging that he is king not by some inherent right or personal achievement but solely because God had "shown great and steadfast love" to David (v. 6). "Steadfast love" *(hesed)* is the commitment that maintains the integrity of a covenant relationship. David had been true to his covenant obligations by walking before the LORD in "faithfulness" *(emet),* "righteousness" *(tsedaqah),* and "uprightness of heart" *(yishrat lebab).* That is, David lived in steadfast commitment ("faithfulness") to God. His deeds corresponded to the standards of right required for the fulfillment of his responsibilities as king ("righteousness"). And he had singleness of purpose ("uprightness of heart," literally, "straightness of heart"). Because of David's integrity God honored his covenant commitment and gave David "a son to sit on his throne this day" (cf. 2 Sam. 7:12). Solomon's acknowledgment adds a new dimension to the understanding of 1 Kgs. 1. The real force shaping the outcome of events there was the covenant faithfulness of God and David.

Solomon's knowledge that he owes his kingship to the covenant faithfulness of God and David heightens his awareness of his own inadequacy. He is as "a little child" who does not know how "to go out or come in" (3:7). Solomon was married to Pharaoh's daughter, and when he began to reign he had a son one year old (11:42; 14:21), so that Solomon was not a "little child" chronologically. Nor is Solomon's behavior in ch. 2 that of a child. "Little child" in this context is the language of humility expressing Solomon's sense of his inexperience and dependence. "To go out and to come in" refers to life beyond the doors of one's household and the city gate in the discharge of one's duties (Deut. 31:2; 1 Sam. 18:16). In Solomon's case this idiom expresses his inexperience and incompetence in the duties and responsibilities of a king.

Solomon is concerned about his inexperience and incompetence because of the special character of the people he is to govern (1 Kgs. 3:8). They are not his people to do with as he pleases. They are God's people, a "chosen" (Deut. 7:6-8), covenanted people ("thy people"), called to be a kingdom of priests and a holy nation (Exod. 19:3-6), God's instrument of blessing to all the families of the earth (Gen. 12:1-3). And they are now a vastly numerous people. They have become the great multitude of descendants promised to Abraham, Isaac, and Jacob. Because of this they are in a strategic position to fulfill their destiny. This people exists not to help Solomon realize his ambitions and self-interest as king but to fulfill their destiny as the covenant people of God. God's covenant with David (1 Kgs. 3:6) is for the sake of implementing his covenant with Israel (v. 8).

Throughout his remarks Solomon refers to David and himself as God's servants (vv. 6, 7, 8). The Hebrew term 'ebed has a wider meaning than the English equivalent, ranging from one who is literally a slave to one who represents and acts for another in a position of responsibility and honor, as Abraham's servant who secured a wife for Isaac (Gen. 24). It is in this latter sense that "servant" is used here. When Solomon refers to David and himself as God's servants, he means that they are not monarchs with absolute, arbitrary power but that they are responsible to God as the implementors of his purposes.

Solomon's request, informed by remembrance and self-examination, is for "an understanding mind to govern thy people, that I may discern between good and evil" (1 Kgs. 3:9a). God restates Solomon's request in v. 11 as "understanding to discern what is right." And when God grants the request he says, "Behold, I give you a wise and discerning mind" (v. 12). All three statements must be taken into account if we are to understand properly Solomon's request.

The phrase "understanding mind" in Hebrew is literally "hearing heart," and this may be the best translation. The heart *(leb)* in Israelite thought is the center of the psychic self. It includes especially mental activity but is broader in scope than English "mind," embracing the feelings and will as well. The heart is susceptible to become hardened, to be made fat (Isa. 6:10), and to dwell on evil (Gen. 6:5; 8:21); indeed, it is "deceitful above all things" (Jer. 17:9). It is over against these capabilities of the heart that Solomon's request is to be understood. A "hearing heart" is one that is open, receptive, teachable (Isa. 50:4). That to which the heart of the king should be open above all else is God's *torah*. The king ideally rules not on the basis of his own understanding but administers his realm in the light of God's revealed will.

Solomon asks for an "understanding mind" ("hearing heart") that he may "govern" God's covenant people. The word translated "govern," *shaphat,* also means "to judge," a meaning preferred by the KJV, NASB, and NJV. The king in Israel did exercise a judicial function (2 Sam. 12:5-6; 14; 15:1-6; 2 Kgs. 8:3; Ps. 72; 122:5; Isa. 11:3-4; 16:5; Jer. 21:12), but the context here favors the meaning "govern." While it is true that Solomon's first act after the experience at Gibeon was to arbitrate a dispute between two mothers (1 Kgs. 3:16-28), this judicial act is followed by an account of his administration and building activities, not by a series of legal disputes. Solomon's task as king is more than judging in the narrow sense. Still, had the intent been to express only the idea of governing, there are other words that express this thought unambiguously *(mashal, malak)*. The choice of *shaphat* means that "justice" should be heard echoing in the translation "govern"— that "govern" in this context is the exercise of authority that makes for justice.

In the final part of his request Solomon asks for the ability to "discern between good and evil." In the practical affairs of government, decisions must be made between conflicting evidence and arguments, between good and bad policies and practices. A "hearing heart," a heart open to and informed by God's *torah,* enables one to distinguish right from wrong, good from evil (cf. Lev. 27:33). God's restatement of Solomon's request in 1 Kgs. 3:11 sheds additional light: "Because you have asked . . . understanding to discern [literally, 'to hear'] what is right ['justice,' *mishpat*]." The purpose of discerning between good and evil is that justice may prevail. This conception of a ruler's responsibility echoes the special nuance of *shaphat* for "govern." Nowhere in the Bible is the moral responsibility of government stated more clearly.

Solomon concludes his request with a rhetorical question: "For who is able to govern this thy great people?" (v. 9b; cf. Deut. 1:9-18). Implicit in the question is the fundamental reason Solomon asked for an understanding mind to govern. He knows that human resources alone are not sufficient for his task. He needs divine empowerment.

3:10-15a *God's Answer.* A choice for one thing is a choice against other things. Solomon does not mention the alternatives he rejected. God knows and enumerates them: long life, riches, and victory over enemies (1 Kgs. 3:11). Each of these is universally prized, especially by a ruler. However, they are not the means of good government, but its by-product. Because Solomon knew what to ask for and what to reject, God is pleased, grants his request—and exceeds it. In addition to "a wise and discerning mind" (v. 12), God gives Solomon riches and honor as well (v. 13). God also promises Solomon long life, but on the condition that Solomon's moral conduct measure up to that of David (v. 14).

The revelatory experience comes to an end with Solomon awakening, aware that "it was a dream." It was precisely through a dream that Solomon sought God. God had honored his quest!

3:15b *Solomon's Return to Jerusalem.* This passage ends as it began, with a journey and sacrifices. Solomon returns to Jerusalem to celebrate God's gifts in a worship service before the ark. Apparently the general public was not invited, for only Solomon's "servants" (i.e., royal officials) are named as being present. Only the sacrifices and a banquet are mentioned, but the context implies that Solomon used this occasion to make known what had happened at Gibeon. He knows himself now to be divinely empowered. He is ready properly to begin his kingship.

THEOLOGICAL REFLECTIONS ON 3:4-15

Solomon's response to God's invitation to "ask what I shall give you" serves as a model for bringing our requests to God. Before asking—and it is proper to ask, for God invites it—one needs to recall what God has already done in one's life. One also needs to evaluate the purpose for which one asks. Is it to further private self-interest or for the furtherance of God's kingdom? Solomon sought first the kingdom (Matt. 6:33), and God added to this riches and honor as well. Finally, Solomon asks not for God to do his work for him, but to be empowered to do it himself.

While this passage is about preparation for kingship, it is also relevant to preparation for leadership in general. The first requirement of leadership is to recognize the need for divine help and to seek it intentionally. It is important to face and acknowledge one's limitations and not to pretend to a competence one does not possess. One leads best who approaches the responsibilities of leadership as a servant who is concerned to enable others to fulfill their God-given destiny. Lastly, one could scarcely improve on Solomon's request for a hearing heart. The heart is the most complex and unmanageable of all the centers of the spiritual life (cf. 1 Kgs. 8:58; Ps. 51:10; Ezek. 36:26). Whatever one does in life, one will do it best if one has a hearing heart.

The ideal of kingship presented in this passage contains some basic guidelines for good government in general. First, government is under God and responsible to God. Second, the governed are God's people, not the state's. Third, the essence of good government is the exercise of authority that makes for justice based on the proper discernment between good and evil. Fourth, the best preparation to govern, undergirding all technical expertise, is a hearing heart, a heart that is sensitive and obedient to God and responsive to the rights and needs of the governed.

SOLOMON SETTLES A DISPUTE BETWEEN TWO MOTHERS (3:16-28)

An opportunity for Solomon to demonstrate the divine gift he received at Gibeon comes when two harlots bring their case to him for settlement. The two women lived in the same house and gave birth to baby boys only three days apart. One mother slept on her baby, suffocating him, and in the night swapped him for the living son of her companion.

The case was especially difficult because each mother claimed the living baby and there were no witnesses. In such cases, recourse was normally made for an answer from God by casting lots, or by an oath of purgation (Exod. 22:10-11), or by ordeal (Num. 5:11-28). Resort to such measures was unnecessary in this case, however, because of Solomon's gift at Gibeon! Solomon hears the two contending women patiently and then draws out the truth by a bold stratagem on the basis of a precedent found in Exod. 21:35. Solomon initially rules to divide the disputed child between the two mothers. By this ruling he puts the two women to the acid test of motherhood, identifies the true mother, and so arrives at the correct ruling.

A similar story is found in many other cultures, and it is no longer possible to determine the original. Whatever its origin, the present story fittingly illustrates the quality of heart and mind with which Solomon was gifted at Gibeon. The understanding mind and the ability to distinguish between good and evil of 1 Kgs. 3:9-12 are here identified as "the wisdom of God" (v. 28). It was so powerfully present in Solomon that the people stood in awe of him.

THEOLOGICAL REFLECTIONS ON 3:16-28

The equitable administration of justice has always been a problem for government. All too often justice is turned into wormwood (Amos 5:7) by favoritism, bias, and the manipulation of the law by the privileged and powerful. The point of this story is that justice is foremost among the responsibilities of government and that justice should be available to all. That Solomon hears the case of the two harlots means that everyone should have access to justice and should be able to present his or her case to the highest authority. Those who govern also have the duty, like Solomon, to take the time and to find the ways and means to establish true justice.

The story is a study of character and motherhood by comparison and contrast. One mother through negligence caused the death of her son, stole the son of another woman, falsely and arrogantly asserted to the king that the boy was hers, and was willing for him to be cut in two rather than surrender him. She wanted a child to possess, and if she could not possess him she was not willing for anyone else to have him. The true mother, because "her heart yearned for her son," was willing to give up her "born one" (*yalud,* a rare word that recalls the experience of birth) that he might live (1 Kgs. 3:26). True love regards the loved one as a gift to be cherished, not a possession to be grasped.

SOLOMON THE
ADMINISTRATOR
1 Kings 4:1-34

The context is the key to the understanding of ch. 4. The action taken here is directly related to the gift of leadership (3:4-15). Solomon's first step to shape his administration was to reorganize the government he inherited from David. This laid the foundation for an ambitious building program, the chief accomplishment of which was the temple.

4:1-6 *Solomon's Cabinet Officers.* David's cabinet consisted of a commander of the volunteer army, a recorder, two high priests, a secretary, and a commander of the royal bodyguard (2 Sam. 8:15-18). An officer in charge of forced labor was later added (2 Sam. 20:24). Solomon combined all the military forces under one head, made the high priesthood a single office, and expanded the office of the secretary to include two officials. He also introduced the offices of superintendent of taxation, king's friend (but cf. 2 Sam. 15:37), and an administrator of the palace (cf. 1 Kgs. 18:3-5; 2 Kgs. 15:5; 18:18; Isa. 36:3).

All these are modest changes except one. The introduction of a cabinet officer in charge of taxation was a radical innovation. For the first time in Israel's history, a state tax was introduced and all the people were brought under the control of a central governmental bureaucracy.

4:7-19 *Solomon's "Bureau of Internal Revenue."* Because it was such a fundamental change, the system of taxation is singled out for additional treatment. The country was divided into twelve districts, and each was administered by a royal official (possibly Gad should be read for Gilead in 1 Kgs. 4:19, following the LXX; cf. v. 13 and JB).

These districts correspond roughly but not precisely to the old tribal territories. The differences are probably due to the incorporation of remaining Canaanite cities and to practical administrative considerations. Whether intentional or not, the new organization was an encroachment of royal authority and the beginning of the erosion of tribal identity.

A curious feature of the roster of names is that for five administrators the first name is missing (vv. 8-11, 13; the "ben" of Ben-hur, Ben-deker, etc., means "son of"). Most likely this is because the text was damaged (cf. JB and 1 Sam. 13:1). The background of the officials who can be identified is impressive. Ben-abinadab (1 Kgs. 4:11) may have been a nephew of David (1 Sam. 16:8), and Ahimaaz (1 Kgs. 4:15) was most likely the son of Zadok (2 Sam. 15:27). Both were sons-in-law of Solomon. The Hushai who was the father of Baana (1 Kgs. 4:16) was undoubtedly the trusted advisor of David (2 Sam. 15:37). Such eminent personages attest the prestigious nature of the office of tax administrator.

The duties of the tax administrators were to supply provisions for one month of the year for the king and his household (1 Kgs. 4:7), to provide barley and straw for the royal chariot force (vv. 27-28), to raise revenue for foreign exchange (5:11), and probably to conscript the labor force for Solomon's construction projects (5:13-18).

Apparently Judah was not included in this taxation system. If Judah had been included, there would have been a total of thirteen districts, but according to 4:7 there were only twelve. Curiously, the "one officer in the land of Judah" (v. 19b) is not named. Is this because the duties of this post were included in those of one of the cabinet officers, as one of the secretaries, the recorder, or the one in charge of the palace? Separate taxation for Judah would have been perceived to be—or would have lent itself to—preferential treatment and would account for the complaint of the northern tribes that Solomon made their yoke heavy (12:4). If Judah was taxed separately, "all Israel" in 4:7 refers to the northern tribes.

4:22-23 *The Provisions for Solomon's Table.* The effectiveness of the new tax system is illustrated by a catalogue of the provisions for Solomon's table for one day. One ox and six sheep fed one hundred and fifty people at Nehemiah's table (Neh. 5:17-18). The "ten fat oxen, and twenty pasture-fed cattle, a hundred sheep, besides harts, gazelles, roebucks, and fatted fowl" (1 Kgs. 4:23) supplied daily to Solomon would have fed many more. These provisions would not have been confined to the royal household, but would have included administrative officials and their households, military personnel, pensioners like Barzillai's sons (2:7), and servants.

4:20-21, 24-25 *The "Good Old Days" of Solomon.* The sumptuous menu of 4:22-23 is framed by two notes, vv. 20-21 and vv. 24-25, elicited from persons who look back on Solomon's reign and recall with nostalgia the power, security, and good life Israel enjoyed at that time. The late date of vv. 24-25 is disclosed by the designation of Solomon's empire as "all the region west of the Euphrates," which presupposes the point of view of one living east of the Euphrates, probably in exile (cf. 2 Sam. 10:16; Neh. 2:7).

1 Kgs. 4:20-21 pictures those halcyon days as characterized by a vast population, a prosperous, carefree life, and Israelite dominion over all of the kingdoms from the Euphrates to the Egyptian border, the extent of David's empire generously reckoned (2 Sam. 8). 1 Kgs. 4:24-25 parallels vv. 20-21 with special emphasis on the peace and security in which Judah and Israel dwelt, "every man under his vine and under his fig tree" (this proverbial expression is also found in 2 Kgs. 18:31; Mic. 4:4; Zech. 3:10). These notes are poignant testimonies of a later generation deprived of a homeland, reduced in numbers, and subject to foreign domination. They could see more clearly than Solomon's contemporaries how blessed they had been.

4:26-28 *Solomon's Chariot Force.* Solomon's new tax system enabled him to maintain a large chariot force stationed at strategic cities throughout his kingdom. Thus the peace and security enjoyed by Israel were buttressed by a strong military establishment (cf. 1 Kgs. 9:15b-19; 10:26-29).

4:29-34 *Solomon's Wisdom.* The good life in Solomon's kingdom also consisted of the pursuit of wisdom, and the one who set the example in this quest was Solomon. Wisdom has more than one meaning. Here it is coordinated with "understanding" and "largeness of mind" and its subject matter embraces the entire range of plant and animal life. Wisdom may be defined in this context as breadth of learning and the ability to gain insight from the observation of nature (cf. Prov. 25:1). Because of such wisdom, Solomon was sought out by "all peoples" and "all the kings of the earth."

THEOLOGICAL REFLECTIONS ON 4:1-34

Building upon the foundation laid by David, Solomon changed fundamentally the structure and quality of life in Israel from that of the days of the judges and the tribal confederacy. It was a change that inevitably provokes controversy. Israel itself was of a divided mind about the virtues of kingship and was well aware of the danger inherent in a strong centralized government (1 Sam. 8; 12). In approaching this subject it is best to avoid extremes. There is a temptation to romanticize the period of the tribal confederacy. For all its democratic virtues, that was also a time when "every man did what was right in his own eyes" (Judg. 17:6; 21:25; cf. 18:1; 19:1; and the grisly episode of the Levite and his concubine at Gibeah in ch. 19). The power to control and tax is a force for good or evil, depending on the way it is used. Without the ability to marshal the resources of the state, Solomon could not have carried out his building program. The immediate context directs us to understand Solomon's reorganization of his government as the product of the gift of leadership granted to him at Gibeon. The larger context instructs us that when God's gift is abused the consequences can be tragic (1 Kgs. 11–12).

SOLOMON THE BUILDER
1 Kings 5:1–9:25

SOLOMON'S TREATY WITH KING HIRAM OF TYRE
(5:1-12)

For all the resources placed at Solomon's disposal by his reorganization of the government, two important essentials were lacking: timber and skilled craftsmen. Both were possessed in abundance by the neighboring kingdom of Tyre. Moreover, Hiram, king of Tyre, had been an ally of David, and his craftsmen had built David's palace (2 Sam. 5:11-12). At the earliest opportunity Solomon renews friendly relations with Tyre and negotiates an agreement to secure timber. Now we learn the real motive for the reorganization of the government. It was that Solomon might finance his building projects.

5:1 *Hiram's Delegation.* It was the custom in the biblical world for monarchs to send a delegation on the occasion of the death of a friend and ally (2 Sam. 10). To do so was to "deal loyally" (*'asah hesed,* 2 Sam. 10:2) with a deceased treaty partner. Such an occasion was a time for condolences and congratulations and for renewing the treaty *(berit)* with the new king. Thus when David died King Hiram of Tyre sent a delegation to Jerusalem, "for Hiram always loved David." In this context "loved" *(ahab)* has a political sense. Hiram had been a faithful ally of David.

The treaty between Tyre and Israel was mutually beneficial. Tyre, emerging as the leading Phoenician kingdom at this time, was the commercial intermediary to the Mediterranean world. Israel was primarily agricultural but also controlled the inland trade routes linking Europe, Asia, and Africa.

5:2-6 *Solomon's Proposal to Secure Timber.* Solomon takes advantage of the presence of the Tyrian delegation to send a message to Hiram expressing his desire to purchase timber so that he might build "a house for the name of the LORD." Since Solomon used the occasion of his accession as sole king to make this request to Hiram, the intention to build the temple was in his mind from the outset of his reign.

From Solomon's message to Hiram we also learn his reasons for building the temple. It was an opportune time. David had intended to build a house for the LORD but was prevented from doing so because he was preoccupied with warfare (1 Kgs. 5:3; contrast 2 Sam. 7:1-11; 1 Chr. 22:8; 28:2-3). Solomon, however, enjoyed peace: "But now the LORD my God has given me rest on every side; there is neither adversary nor misfortune" (1 Kgs. 5:4). Credit is given to God for these conditions, but Solomon deserves some recognition as well. His alliance with Egypt was fundamental to the harmonious political climate. It is also to Solomon's credit that he did not succumb to the lure of militarism. With Israel as the strongest power in Palestine-Syria, it must have been a temptation to Solomon to extend his sway. If so, he resisted it. His first priority was to build a temple for the LORD.

One does not build a temple for the LORD out of private ambition and because of favorable conditions. Such an undertaking requires a divine mandate. Solomon had received such a mandate through the prophecy of Nathan, and he freely cites the prophet's words to this effect: "Your [David's] son, whom I will set upon your throne in your place, shall build the house for my name" (v. 5; cf. 2 Sam. 7:12-13). Nathan's prophecy authorizes and obligates Solomon to build a temple for the LORD. This prophecy also supports the legitimacy of Solomon as the proper successor of David (cf. 1 Kgs. 1:48; 2:15, 24; 3:6-7).

As compensation for the timber from Lebanon, Solomon proposes to pay the wages of Hiram's workers but does not name the kind and amount, leaving that to Hiram (5:6). For good measure, Solomon volunteers to send Israelites to help the Tyrian workers, who were famous as timber cutters.

5:7-9 *Hiram's Response.* Hiram recognizes in Solomon's intention to build a temple the evidence of his wisdom and of God's providence in providing David with such a son. This is another inadvertent testimony to the propriety of Solomon's succession and is especially noteworthy as coming from a foreign observer.

Hiram accepts Solomon's request for timber, promises him as much as he desires, and sets forth his terms (vv. 8-9). Ignoring the offer of Israelite workers, Hiram states that his labor force would cut and float cedar and cypress down the Mediterranean coast to a place designated by Solomon (Joppa, according to 2 Chr. 2:16). Hiram also specifies that compensation is to be in the form of provisions of food for his household and is to be paid directly to him rather than to his laborers. In this way Hiram maintains control over the revenue from Solomon.

5:10-12 *Implementation of the Agreement.* Solomon accepts Hiram's terms and in return for "all the cedar and cypress he desired" pays Hiram annually about 4,400 kiloliters (125,000 bushels) of wheat and about 440 kiloliters (115,000 gallons, reading "bath" with LXX; cf. NIV; TEV) of "beaten" olive oil. Beaten oil was processed by beating with a hand-pestle in a mortar. (Ordinary olive oil was produced by crushing the olives in large stone presses, with resulting debris.) Apparently these payments were maintained throughout the first twenty years of Solomon's building program (1 Kgs. 9:10-11).

A concluding interpretive comment directs the reader to the proper understanding of Solomon's agreement with Hiram: "And the LORD gave Solomon wisdom, as he promised him" (5:12a). God's gift of wisdom refers, of course, to the promise made to Solomon at Gibeon (3:10-12). The twofold reference to Solomon's wisdom (5:7, 12) means that the agreement with Hiram should be seen as the fruit of a hearing heart to govern.

THEOLOGICAL REFLECTIONS ON 5:1-12

Foreign influence is regarded throughout 1–2 Kings as a serious threat to Israel's identity and existence. Yet Solomon's initiative to a pagan king to obtain the timber for Israel's most sacred sanctuary is affirmed as an expression of divine wisdom (cf. v. 18 and 7:13-46)! Moreover, Solomon and Hiram made a treaty *(berit)* and peace *(shalom,* harmonious goodwill) prevailed between them

(5:12b). This passage is a reminder of the delicate relationship of Israel (and the Church) to the world. While Israel is not to be identified with the world, it is still God's world and God works through it as well as through the covenant people. Israel's (and the Church's) mission is not to condemn or to escape from the world but to transform it. That mission needs help from those outside as well as within the covenant relationship.

SOLOMON'S LABOR FORCE (5:13-18)

The remaining task for Solomon to implement his building program was to raise a large labor force. The treatment of this undertaking is brief and disjointed. The present passage is paralleled by 9:15-23, which gives both supplementary and conflicting evidence.

5:13-14 *Timber Workers.* Hiram at first declined Solomon's offer of Israelite workers (5:9). Apparently there was some modification in the terms of the agreement, for Solomon conscripted a contingent of 30,000 timber workers who were required to give three months of the year in service to the state. Under the authority of the cabinet officer, Adoniram (4:6), they were divided into three groups and rotated in relays so that each group worked one month in Lebanon and spent two months at home.

5:15-17 *Porters and Hewers of Stone.* In addition to the timber workers, there was an enormous force of burden bearers (70,000) and stonecutters (80,000) "in the hill country" quarrying the limestone with which Palestine abounds. They were administered separately from the timber workers by some 3,300 "chief officers" (cf. 9:23). There is no mention of relief from this service through rotation. While the timber workers came "out of all Israel" (5:13), the place of origin of the burden bearers and stonecutters is not given. Most likely they were the descendants of "all the people who were left of the Amorites, the Hittites, the Perizzites, the Hivites, and the Jebusites" whom Solomon made a "forced levy of slaves" (9:20-21), that is, subjected to permanent service.

5:18 *Summary.* A concluding summary links this disparate aggregate of Israelite and Phoenician workers into a single task force united by the common objective of preparing the timber and stones for the temple. It was their shared skills and joint effort that made the construction of the temple possible.

THEOLOGICAL REFLECTIONS ON 5:13-18

Forced labor was an established institution in the biblical world. The Israelites had been subjected to it in Egypt, and it was an accepted part of the culture of the Canaanites now incorporated into Solomon's empire and of other neighboring peoples. David had introduced forced labor into Israel late in his reign but on a modest scale. Solomon expanded it to such a degree that it must have involved virtually everyone in his kingdom. A distinction was made between Israelites and non-Israelites. For Israelites it was a temporary service limited to a few months out of the year (9:22). For the descendants of the subjugated Canaanites it was a permanent obligation. Forced labor continued throughout the history of the Israelite state, but not on the scale employed by Solomon.

As with the building of the cathedrals of Europe, Solomon's laborers may well have begun their work with joy, enthusiasm, and a sense of building to the glory of God. If so, it is clear that by the end of Solomon's reign this was no longer the case. The northern tribes bore a disproportionate share of the burden in relation to Judah (5:13; 11:26-28; 12:4, 9, 10, 11, 14), and the subjugated Canaanites were treated worst of all (9:20-21). Moreover, Solomon prolonged this service unduly. While the temple, government buildings, and palaces were completed during the first half of Solomon's reign, the protest of the northern tribes indicates that the labor force was kept at or near full strength for the remainder of his reign. How ironic and regrettable that those who had been victimized by forced labor would themselves practice it (cf. 1 Sam. 8:12, 16, 17; Jer. 22:13).

THE CONSTRUCTION OF THE TEMPLE, ADJACENT BUILDINGS, AND TEMPLE FURNISHINGS (6:1–7:51)

The building of the temple is the centerpiece of the history of Solomon's reign. As such it is treated in greater detail than any other achievement. 1 Kgs. 6 and 7, in fact, are the fullest description of a temple and its furnishings from the biblical world. Still, many questions remain unanswered, for the account is highly selective and full of obscure architectural terminology. Fortunately, chs. 6–7 are supplemented by the parallel version in 2 Chr. 3:1–5:1, Ezekiel's vision of the temple of the restoration in chs. 40–42 of his prophecy, and archaeological excavations of temples in Palestine-Syria and other parts of the ancient Near East.

The treatment of the temple in 1 Kgs. 6–7 is of a technical nature such as would be of interest to an architect or builder. These chapters record dates, materials used, dimensions, and architectural techniques; descriptive detail is sparse and incidental. In order to help the reader visualize the temple and its furnishings, the writer has treated the text of chs. 6–7 topically and drawn upon Ezekiel's vision and archaeological findings.

6:1, 37-38 *The date of the beginning and completion of the Temple.* Work on the temple was begun in the month of Ziv (Apr.-May) of the fourth year of Solomon's reign. This date reveals how busy and purposeful Solomon was during his first three years. During this time he dealt with the remaining internal threats to his authority, contracted a marriage alliance with Egypt, reorganized his government, negotiated a treaty with Hiram, and made ready a huge labor force—an impressive achievement.

The beginning of Solomon's reign can be determined only approximately. According to the chronology adopted in this work, the date of the division of the monarchy was 931 B.C. (Edwin R. Thiele, *The Mysterious Numbers of the Hebrew Kings;* another widely accepted chronology is that of William F. Albright, "The Chronology of the Divided Monarchy of Israel"; for a comprehensive listing of chronological systems, cf. John H. Hayes and J. Maxwell Miller, eds., *Israelite and Judaean History,* 678-683). Allowing forty years for Solomon's reign (11:42), this would place the beginning of his rule at 971 and the fourth year of his reign at 967. But the forty years may be a round number, and we do not know whether the four years are calculated from the beginning of Solomon's co-regency with David or his sole reign. The date is best assigned to the decade of the 960s without attempting to be precise.

The building of the temple was an event of such magnitude as to place it with the landmarks of Israel's history. It is thus brought into relationship with the Exodus from Egypt and calculated to be the 480th year after that event. It was also 480 years from the building of the temple to the return from the Babylonian Exile. This latter date may be derived by computing the length of the reigns of the kings of Judah supplied by 1–2 Kings, which amount to 430 years, and by adding to this sum the 50 years of the Babylonian Exile. The sum of 480 years from the Exodus to the building of the temple is based on the following calculations according to Martin Noth (*The Deuteronomistic History,* 18-25):

From Moses to the conquest of Transjordan (Deut. 1:3; Josh. 14:10)	45 years
From Othniel (Judg. 3:7-11) to Abdon (Judg. 12:13-15)	350
Philistine oppression (Judg. 13:1)	40
Reign of Saul (1 Sam. 13:1)	2
Reign of David (1 Kgs. 2:11)	40
Solomon's sole reign to building of the temple (assuming Solomon's first year overlaps David's last year).	3
	480 years

The temple was completed in the eighth month of Solomon's eleventh year (1 Kgs. 6:37-38). Thus seven and one-half years (rounded off to seven in v. 38) were devoted to the construction of a building of very modest size. These dates attest both the historic significance of the temple and the care of its construction.

Dimensions and Measurements. The dimensions of the temple are given in cubits, a unit of measure based on the distance between the elbow and the tip of the index finger. Since these measurements vary with individuals, different cubits were in use: the common cubit (Deut. 3:11), the old standard cubit (2 Chr. 3:3), and the royal cubit, which was a cubit and a handbreadth (Ezek. 40:5; 43:13). On the basis of the measurement of Hezekiah's tunnel (2 Kgs. 20:20), which according to the Siloam inscription was 1,200 cubits long, the cubit used there has been calculated to be 44.45 cm. or 17.49 inches. For the purposes of this study this cubit is assumed to be the one used for the temple. For the sake of convenience it is rounded off to 18 in., and the equivalent of cubits is given in feet (cf. TEV). So reckoned, the basic edifice of the temple was a rectangular structure 90 ft. long, 30 ft. wide, and 45 ft. high according to its inner measurements (1 Kgs. 6:2, 20). Around this core, side chambers were built reaching approximately midway of the central edifice.

Foundation Platform and Stone Work. The temple rested on a stone foundation platform 9 ft. high and projecting beyond the walls of the temple 7.5 ft., giving a sense of height and grandeur. The temple edifice was made of "costly stones, hewn according to measure, sawed with saws, back and front, even from the foundation to the coping" (1 Kgs. 7:9). (The limestone of Palestine is soft until exposed to the elements.) The foundation stones were especially large, 12 to 15 ft. long (v. 10). The outer walls of the side chambers were 7.5 ft. thick (Ezek. 41:9).

Jachin and Boaz. The temple faced east (1 Kgs. 7:39; Ezek. 8:16; 11:1; 43:1-4; 44:1-3; 47:1) and one entered it by climbing a flight of ten steps (Ezek. 40:49). Flanking the entrance were two tremendous, freestanding bronze pillars named Jachin and Boaz (1 Kgs. 7:15-22). Their hollow shafts, "four fingers" thick, were 18 ft. in circumference and 27 ft. high. Crowning them were bowl-shaped capitals 7.5 ft. high. The capitals were decorated with a molded relief checkerboard pattern, sheathed by huge lily-like leaves. Two garlands of pomegranates, one hundred to a strand, were festooned about each capital. Four of these were attached, and the others hung free (Jer. 52:23). The capitals were covered with gratings.

The function of these pillars and the significance of their names are nowhere explained. Apart from the account of their confiscation by the Babylonians after the sack of Jerusalem (2 Kgs. 25:13, 16-17), they are mentioned elsewhere only in connection with two ceremonial occasions. At the time of his coronation, Joash stood "by the pillar, according to the custom" (2 Kgs. 11:14), and Josiah "stood by the pillar" when he made a covenant with the people (2 Kgs. 23:3). These are intriguing bits of information but scarcely provide a solution to the function of these pillars. Nor are their names self-explanatory. Jachin means "he will establish" and Boaz "in strength." A number of examples of freestanding pillars at the entrance of temples have been found in Phoenicia and elsewhere in the biblical world. They were thus a traditional feature of temple architecture.

Among the many suggestions that have been made as to the significance of these pillars, the following may be mentioned: they were altars where the fat of the sacrifice or incense was burned (note the gratings at the tops); they represented the pillar of cloud and the pillar of fire that guided Israel in the wilderness; they were stylized versions of the stone pillar and sacred tree or pole central to the high place sanctuaries; they symbolized the tree of life; they were markers of the equinoxes, the temple being so oriented that the rays of the sun shone directly into the inner sanctuary at the fall and spring equinox; they were Egyptian-style obelisks; they represented the two pillars of the Israelite state, God and king; they were witnesses of the covenant after the analogy of the standing stones in Josh. 24:26-27; they were simply conventional imitations of contemporary temple architecture and decorative only. The most plausible suggestion in the judgment of the writer is that these pillars were markers of the equinoxes. An accurate calendar was important to priests for determining the sacred seasons, the temple was oriented to the east, and at the dedication of the temple Solomon was concerned to avoid any confusion between God and the sun (1 Kgs. 8:12-13; cf. 2 Kgs. 23:11; Ezek. 8:16).

With regard to the significance of the names of the pillars, one of the most attractive suggestions to date is that of R. B. Y. Scott ("The Pillars of Jachin and Boaz"), who suggests that they were the initial words of inscriptions relating to David and his dynasty (note the association of the king with these pillars in 2 Kgs. 11:14; 23:3). Jachin ("he will establish") may have begun an inscription such as "*He* [God] *will establish* the throne of David and his kingdom, to his seed forever," and Boaz ("in strength") may have been the first words of "*In the strength* of the LORD shall the king rejoice." These names are capable of other explanations, of course, and Scott's suggestion must be regarded as tentative.

Vestibule (ulam). Passing between Jachin and Boaz, one entered the vestibule. It was 30 ft. wide, 15 ft. long (1 Kgs. 6:3), and was constructed of three courses of hewn stone to one course of cedar beams (7:12). Its height is not given, nor is there mention of a ceiling, doors, decoration, or furniture. Ezekiel's temple had an entrance 21 ft. wide (Ezek. 40:48). Because of the paucity of information about the vestibule, it is uncertain whether it was an enclosed area or an open porch.

Nave (hekal). From the vestibule one entered the nave, a room 30 by 60 ft., through massive doors of cypress decorated with carved palm trees, cherubim, and open flowers (1 Kgs. 6:33-35), and plated with gold (2 Kgs. 18:16). The doors were so massive—15 ft. wide (Ezek. 41:2)—that each was divided into two folding leaves. According to 1 Kgs. 7:50, they were fitted into sockets of gold.

In contrast to temples in Mesopotamia and Egypt, the interior of the stone edifice of Solomon's temple was finished with wood. The nave was floored with cypress, panelled with cedar (6:15), and ceiled with cedar beams crossed at right angles forming hollow squares which were finished with cedar boards (v. 9b). The panelled walls were decorated with carved gourds, open flowers, cherubim, and palm trees (vv. 18, 29). The palm trees divided the wall into panels within which was a cherub with two faces, a human face looking in one direction and a lion face looking in the other (Ezek. 41:17-20). The flowers and gourds should probably be visualized as in garlands strung from palm tree to palm tree. This pattern ran around both the nave and inner sanctuary "from the floor to above the door" (Ezek. 41:20). The carvings were inlaid with gold; indeed, the "whole house" (1 Kgs. 6:21, 22a), even the floors (v. 30), are said to have been overlaid (or thinly gilded) with gold. Ezekiel does not mention goldwork in his description of the temple.

The nave was lighted by windows near the ceiling (6:4). "Recessed frames," if this is the correct translation, suggests that they had large interior openings that tapered to small exteriors so as to make possible the maximum of light with a minimum of exposure to the elements (cf. Ezek. 40:16). Probably they were provided with protective gratings.

The furniture of the nave consisted of ten golden lampstands, a cedar incense altar overlaid with gold (1 Kgs. 6:20b, 22; cf. Exod. 30:1-10), and a table for the bread of the Presence (1 Kgs. 7:48). Five lampstands were placed on each side of the room. The incense altar stood before the entrance to the inner sanctuary (v. 49; cf. 6:22).

The Inner Sanctuary (debir). A wooden partition (contrast Ezek. 41:3) built at the rear of the temple created the most holy place or holy of holies. It was a cube, 30 ft. in each of its dimensions. Since its height was 15 ft. less than the rest of the temple, it was either on a raised platform or a loft was built above it. There were no windows. The purpose of the inner sanctuary was to house "the ark of the covenant of the LORD" (1 Kgs. 6:19), the sacred emblem of God's immanent, sacramental presence. It is this function that defines the meaning and significance of the temple and accounts for its rather modest dimensions. It was built to house God's presence, not a worshipping congregation.

Whether on the same level as the nave or elevated and reached by stairs, the inner sanctuary was entered through doors made of olivewood shaped in the form of a pentagon (6:31). That is, the doorposts angled out from the floor and were peaked at the top. Was this shape chosen to suggest a tent, and was olivewood chosen to preserve an association with the wilderness?

Within the inner sanctuary facing the entrance were two carved cherubim of olivewood overlaid with gold (6:23-28). They had a wing span of 15 ft. and were 15 ft. tall. Cherubim are hybrid creatures with the body of a lion or ox (symbolizing strength), wings (symbolizing mobility), and human faces (symbolizing intelligence). In the OT they appear in two capacities: (1) as guardians of sacred areas (paradise, Gen. 3:24; Ezek. 28:14-16; the mercy seat, Exod. 25:18-20) and (2) as bearers of God's throne (e.g., 1 Sam. 4:4; 2 Sam. 6:2; 22:11 = Ps. 18:10; 2 Kgs. 19:15 = Isa. 37:16; Ezek. 1:4-14). Since the outspread wing of each cherub touched the wall and their inner wings met in the middle of the room (1 Kgs. 6:27; cf. 8:6-7), they are apparently conceived as in flight. If this is correct, they must be thought of here as bearers of God's throne, symbolized by the ark beneath them.

Because it was the most holy part of the temple, the inner sanctuary was not freely accessible to the priesthood. On special occasions the ark was brought forth and carried in procession (e.g., Pss. 24, 132). Otherwise only the high priest, specially bathed and clothed, entered the holy of holies on the Day of Atonement (Lev. 16:2-4, 34).

Side Chambers (yatsi'a). These were a collarlike addition built onto the nave and inner sanctuary but not the vestibule (1 Kgs. 6:5,

10). There were three stories of the side chambers, each a cubit wider than the one beneath so that the floors of the second and third stories were supported by the recessed walls below. The bottom story was 7.5 ft. wide, the middle story 9 ft., and the top story 10.5 ft. (v. 6a). Each story was 7.5 ft. high (v. 10). The number of chambers is not given, but in Ezekiel's temple there were thirty for each floor (Ezek. 41:6). The one entrance (1 Kgs. 6:8) was almost certainly on the outside, for an inner entrance to this utilitarian structure would have violated the sanctity of the temple. (Ezekiel's temple had two entrances to the side chambers, Ezek. 41:11.) No windows are mentioned, but it is difficult to see how the side chambers would have been functional without them.

The side chambers were used for the storage of treasure (1 Kgs. 15:18; 2 Kgs. 12:18; 14:14; 16:8; 18:15), equipment (1 Kgs. 7:40, 45, 49b, 50a), and tithes (Neh. 10:38-39). Here the infant Joash was hidden from the murderous Athaliah (2 Kgs. 11:2-3). An annotator emphasizes that the utilitarian side chambers did not violate the sanctity of the temple. The supporting beams that joined the side chambers to the nave and inner sanctuary were fitted to offsets *on* the wall; they were not inserted *into* the wall (1 Kgs. 6:6b).

Courtyard. The temple was set within a courtyard surrounded by a wall made of three courses of hewn stone to one course of cedar beams (6:36; 7:9b, 12; cf. Ezra 6:4). This was a common form of construction to allow for settling, freezing, thawing, and earthquakes. The courtyard was an extension of the temple and the place of congregational worship (Ps. 43:4; 65:4; 84:2, 10; 100:4; 116:18-19; Isa. 1:12). To be in the courtyard was the same as being in God's house (Ps. 5:7; 135:2).

Altar. The most important object in the courtyard was the altar. It is not mentioned in 1 Kgs. 6–7 because it was not one of Solomon's works but had been erected by David (2 Sam. 24:18-25). Approximately two centuries after the reign of Solomon, King Ahaz replaced the altar of David and Solomon by a larger one in a new style (2 Kgs. 16:10-16). It is Ahaz's altar that is best known because it is presumably the basis of the one described in Ezekiel. According to the account there, the altar was a three-tiered structure 30 ft. square at the base and 15 ft. high with steps to the altar hearth from the east (Ezek. 43:13-17; 2 Chr. 4:1). It was located in the center of the courtyard in front of the temple (1 Kgs. 8:64; 2 Kgs. 16:14; Ezek. 40:47). As representing the deity and the place where sacrifice was offered, it was the focal point of worship (Ps. 26:6-7; 43:4; 118:27).

Molten Sea. After the altar, the most conspicuous object in the courtyard was the molten sea, a huge bronze bowl 7.5 ft. high, 15 ft. in diameter, 45 ft. in circumference, and a "handbreadth" thick (1 Kgs. 7:23-26). (The slight discrepancy in the ratio between the diameter and circumference is either because the measurements are rounded off or because the circumference is taken from an inner and the diameter from an outer measurement.) The molten sea was decorated with two strands of gourds near the rim and supported by twelve bronze bulls arranged in triads, each triad facing one of the cardinal points of the compass (vv. 24-25). It was stationed at the southeastern corner of the temple (v. 39; cf. Ezek. 47:1). Estimated to have weighed 25-30 tons and to have held about 4.5 kiloliters (11,500 gallons) of water, the molten sea was a marvel of craftsmanship. It too was a traditional feature of temple architecture of the time.

Priests have abundant need of water, and this large container obviously served a practical purpose (2 Chr. 4:6; Exod. 30:17-21; 40:30-32; Lev. 16:4, 23-24). Its designation as "sea" suggests that it may have had a symbolic function as well. In the biblical world, especially in Mesopotamia and Palestine-Syria, the sea represented a cosmic power of chaos in nature that periodically threatens all ordered existence and must be subdued in order for life to be possible. Many passages in the Bible indicate that Israel shared this point of view. One of the clearest examples is Ps. 93:3-5:

> The floods have lifted up, O LORD,
> > the floods have lifted up their voice,
> > the floods lift up their roaring.
> Mightier than the thunders of many waters,
> > mightier than the waves of the sea,
> > the LORD on high is mighty!

As well as serving as a reservoir of water for the use of priests, the molten sea may have helped worshippers to visualize this perceived power of chaos as they celebrated God's triumph over it.

The Ten Bronze Water Carts. Positioned on each side of the temple were five bronze water carts. These carts were 6 ft. square, 4.5 ft. high, and the wheels were 2.5 ft. in diameter (1 Kgs. 7:27, 32). The carts were lavishly decorated with lions, oxen, cherubim, and wreaths (vv. 28-29, 36). Each cart cradled a bronze basin 6 ft. in diameter that is estimated to have held about 880 liters (233 gallons). These basins served the practical purpose of making water available to the worshipping congregation to wash in and "to rinse off what was used for the burnt offering" (2 Chr. 4:6; Lev. 1:9, 13).

The Great Rock. The site of the temple is presently occupied by the Moslem sanctuary, the Dome of the Rock, so named because it houses a sacred rock measuring 60 ft. by 40 ft. by 4-6 ft. No mention is made of this rock in the account of the building of the temple nor is it referred to directly elsewhere in the OT. Nevertheless, it occupies a prominent place in Jewish tradition, where it is regarded as "the foundation stone" of heaven and earth (cf. Isa. 28:16-17a; Matt. 16:18; cf. also rock as a metaphor for God, e.g., Deut. 32:4, 15, 18, 30, 31, 37; Ps. 18:2, 31, 46; Isa. 44:8). The massive presence of this rock would inevitably have influenced the layout of the temple grounds. Possibly the stone was considered as holy by the Jebusites and accepted as such by the Israelites (cf. Samuel L. Terrien, "The Omphalos Myth and Hebrew Religion"). It has been variously suggested that the great altar or the inner sanctuary was built upon it or that it stood exposed, either near the great altar or to one side of the temple.

Buildings Adjacent to the Temple. Solomon's architects followed the traditional practice of their time by making the temple part of a larger cluster of buildings including the House of the Forest of Lebanon, Hall of Pillars, Hall of Judgment, Solomon's palace, and the palace for Pharaoh's daughter. According to 1 Kgs. 9:10, these buildings were constructed after the completion of the temple and thirteen years were devoted to them (7:1).

House of the Forest of Lebanon. This is the only building treated in detail. The name derives from the "forest" of cedar pillars used in its construction. The building is impressive in size: 150 ft. long, 75 ft. wide, and 45 ft. high (7:2a). But the configuration of the building's interior, the vantage point of the narrator, is difficult to visualize. Were there three (LXX, RSV, TEV) or four (MT, NEB, JB, NAB, NIV, NJV) rows of cedar pillars (v. 2b)? The three rows of windows (v. 4) suggest three stories. Was the entire building divided into three stories, or was this true only for the side chambers? Nor is the purpose of this building stated. From 10:17 and Isa. 22:8 it may be inferred that a portion of it at least was used for an armory.

Hall of Pillars, Hall of the Throne, Solomon's palace, and the Palace for Pharaoh's Daughter. It is not clear whether the Hall of Pillars and the Hall of the Throne (cf. 1 Kgs. 10:18-20), also called the Hall of Judgment, were separate buildings or porticoes of the House of the Forest of Lebanon (7:6-7). (The length of the Hall of Pillars is identical with the width of the House of the Forest of Lebanon.) The Hall of Judgment (no dimensions given) is tangible evidence of the central role played by the king in the administration of justice (cf. Ps. 122:5). No details are given about Solomon's palace and the palace of Pharaoh's daughter except that they were in a separate court back of "the hall" (of the throne?) and that their construction was of like quality with the other buildings (1 Kgs. 7:8). That only eight verses are devoted to the government buildings and royal palaces is in itself a statement about their importance relative to the temple.

The Temple-palace Complex. The temple, royal palaces, and government buildings were in close proximity to one another but demarcated by courtyards. The "inner court" surrounding the temple (6:36) shared a common wall with the courtyard for the royal palaces (7:8). There was also a "great court" (v. 12) encompassing the government buildings and possibly the entire compound. The narrow eastern ridge of Jerusalem, the site of the temple and the city of David, slopes down in a southeasterly direction to where it abuts above the juncture of the Kidron and Hinnom Valleys. Since one went down from the temple to the king's palace (2 Kgs. 11:19; Jer. 22:1; 36:12; cf. Jer. 26:10), the temple would have been the northernmost building in the group, with the other buildings arranged in a north-south direction.

THEOLOGICAL REFLECTIONS ON 6:1–7:51

The dating of the beginning of work on the temple in relation to the Exodus and the Babylonian Exile is a theological as well as a chronological statement. Theologically, this dating affirms that the temple stands at the heart of Israel's history. The two events to which the temple is related define the range of experiences for which the temple is relevant as reaching from Liberation to Exile. The temple is the proper place to celebrate and interpret the meaning of triumph. It is also the place to take one's sorrows and to find hope in the midst of tragedy. Even those problems that are a wearisome task to understand yield meaning in the sanctuary of God (Ps. 73:16-17).

The work on the temple was done with lavish care. No expense was spared. Only the finest materials were used: costly dressed stones, cedar, and cypress. Extravagant use was made of bronze and gold. Intricate carvings decorated the nave, inner sanctuary, and doors. Skilled carpenters and stone masons were imported from Tyre and Gebal (1 Kgs. 5:18; cf. Ezek. 27:3-9). Hiram of Tyre, who supervised the bronze work, was "full of wisdom, understanding, and skill for making any work in bronze" (1 Kgs. 7:14; cf. Exod. 31:3; 35:31). Moreover, the work was done with reverential dignity free of raucous clamor, for the stones were prepared at the quarry "so that neither hammer nor axe nor any tool of iron was heard in the temple, while it was being built" (1 Kgs. 6:7). Even the amount of time devoted to the construction of a building of such modest size was lavish. Such effort, such skill, such lavish care befits any work devoted to God. Indeed, should not all our work be done as if it were on the temple?

No amount of effort, skill, and care, however, can insure God's presence. At some point during the work on the temple the word of the LORD came to Solomon (through a prophet?), emphatically stating that the condition of God's fulfilling his word to David and even his presence among his people was obedience (6:11-13). This word tempers the pride and reverential regard with which the temple is held in ch. 6 with a warning against presuming that God is bound to the temple. Not a splendid house but obedience is the condition of God's presence.

THE DEDICATION OF THE TEMPLE (8:1–9:9)

This is the most detailed account of a dedication ceremony in the Bible. It is, in effect, a treatise on the theology of God's presence—or perhaps one should say, theologies, for more than one voice is discernible here. A careful reading reveals a history of some four hundred years of Israel's attempt to express its understanding of the nature of the presence of God.

The Installation of the Ark in the Temple (8:1-13)

The first step in the dedication of the temple is the transfer of the ark from the tent "which David had pitched for it" (2 Sam. 6:17) to the inner sanctuary of the temple. It is a delicate undertaking charged with suspense as to whether or not the LORD would find the temple pleasing and accept it.

8:1-3a *Solomon Assembles the People.* The date chosen for this momentous event was "the feast in the month Ethanim" (Sept.-Oct.), that is, the Feast of Ingathering or Booths. This festival, which marked the end of the harvest season and the beginning of the new year, was the most important festival in ancient Israel. The temple had been completed in the eighth month (6:38), but Ethanim was the seventh month (8:2). This means that the dedication of the temple was postponed eleven months so that it might take place at this high point of the religious year. At the appointed time Solomon assembles a great multitude of leaders and representatives of all the people in Jerusalem "to bring up the ark . . . out of the city of David, which is Zion," to the temple built on newly developed land on a higher elevation to the north.

8:3b-11 *The Procession.* Surrounded by Solomon and the assembled throng, the ark begins its short but fateful journey. The procession is attended by numerous sacrifices, probably offered at the very beginning (cf. 2 Sam. 6:12-13), at stations along the way, and particularly at the great altar in the courtyard of the temple. Any untoward happening or rejection of the sacrifices would signal God's disapproval of this move (cf. 2 Sam. 6:1-10). The procession is completed without incident, and the ark is installed in "its place" in the inner sanctuary (1 Kgs. 8:6).

The drama of this moment is prolonged by two digressions. Verses 7-8 describe how the wings of the cherubim made a covering over the ark and how the poles of the ark projected so far beyond it that their ends could be seen from a vantage point just outside the inner sanctuary. Verse 9 states that "there was nothing in the ark except the two tables of stone which Moses put there at Horeb" (contrast Exod. 16:33; Num. 17:10; Heb. 9:4). The interest in these details is not merely archaeological and descriptive. The poles used to carry the ark were deliberately left in place (Exod. 25:15) to emphasize its portable character and the dynamic nature of God's presence. The description of the ark as the container of the Ten Commandments is related to a distinct theology of the divine presence to be developed in 1 Kgs. 8:16-19, 27-30.

It is not until vv. 10-11 that the suspense of the occasion is resolved. A cloud, equated with "the glory of the LORD" (i.e., the perceptible, numinous presence of God), fills the entire temple (cf. Exod. 40:34-35; Ezek. 43:1-7a). God approves and accepts the new place of his presence!

As a result of God's acceptance of the temple, Jerusalem—also called Zion (1 Kgs. 8:1; 2 Sam. 5:6-9)—assumed a special place among cities (Ps. 87:1-3). It came to be regarded as the holy city, the mother of Israel and symbol of Israel's identity. A special hymnody grew up celebrating Zion, the "Songs of Zion" (Pss. 46, 48, 76, 87; cf. also 84, 122, 132). This is why 1–2 Kings insists that Jerusalem was the only proper and legitimate place of worship.

8:12-13 *Solomon's Dedicatory Remarks.* As the builder of the temple, Solomon formally offers the temple to God. The significance of the event is stated in an address to the people employing two striking contrasts (1 Kgs. 8:12). The first contrast is between God and the sun. The sun, so far removed yet vital to life, serves to dramatize the far greater "distance" and power of God for whom the sun is a small object which he placed in the heavens. The One who consents to make himself present in the temple is the Creator and majestic sovereign of the universe. The second contrast is between light and darkness. Whereas the sun is characterized by brightness, God has chosen to dwell in thick darkness. This refers in the first instance to the inner sanctuary, which had no windows. Darkness is also used in a symbolic sense to express the truth that though the Lord of the sun and of light graciously consents to make himself present in the temple there is an inexhaustible mystery and depth to his being that remains concealed.

Verse 13 is addressed directly to God, formally conferring the temple to him. Solomon identifies himself as the builder of the temple and states that he has built it expressly for the LORD as "a place for thee to dwell in for ever."

The Different Voices of the Passage. The closer one looks at vv. 1-13 the more one becomes aware that they do not speak with one voice. A remarkably varied vocabulary is used to denote the assembled throng: "the elders of Israel and all the heads of the tribes, the leaders of the fathers' houses of the people of Israel" (v. 1), "all the men of Israel" (v. 2), "all the elders of Israel" (v. 3), "all the congregation of Israel" (v. 5). Verse 1 states that the elders were assembled to bring up the ark, but it was the priests who actually did so (vv. 3b, 6, 10, 11) or the priests and the Levites (v. 4). Nor is there uniform designation of the ark. It is sometimes "the ark" or "the ark of the LORD" (vv. 3b, 4, 5, 9) and at other times "the ark of the covenant of the LORD" (vv. 1, 6).

There are also indications that this passage in its present form took shape over a long period of time. The distinction between priests and Levites did not arise until after the Babylonian Exile (587 B.C.). Until that time all Levites were full-fledged priests. After the Exile only descendants of Aaron had the privilege of sacrifice; all other Levites were restricted to being singers and menial attendants (see above on 2:26-27, 35b). Also "congregation of Israel" (v. 5) is a usage that became current only during and after the Exile.

Finally, three distinct voices can be heard speaking about the nature of the ark. According to one voice the ark was God's portable throne on which he was invisibly present (1 Sam. 4:4, 6-7), and it was so charged with holiness that to look into it or to touch it incurred death (1 Sam. 6:19-20; 2 Sam. 6:6-7). God's presence was so closely associated with the ark according to this conception that "Whenever the ark set out, Moses said, 'Arise, O LORD, and let thy enemies be scattered. . . .' And when it rested, he said, 'Return, O LORD, to the ten thousand thousands of Israel'" (Num. 10:35-36). A gathering of the people before the ark was the same as being "before the LORD" (e.g., Judg. 20:23, 26-27; 21:2). In the liturgy reenacting David's bringing of the ark to Jerusalem, the leader says:

> Arise, O LORD, and go to thy resting place,
> > thou and the ark of thy might. (Ps. 132:8)

While it is the ark that is being brought into the temple in Ps. 24:7-10, emblem and divine presence are so completely identified that no effort is made to distinguish them:

> Lift up your heads, O gates!
> > and be lifted up, O ancient doors!
> > that the King of glory may come in.

It is this understanding of "the ark" or "the ark of the LORD" that makes it possible for Solomon to speak of God dwelling in the temple (1 Kgs. 8:13; cf. Ps. 68:16; 76:2; 132:7, 14; Isa. 6; 8:18; 37:14; Ezek. 37:27; 43:7; 48:35; Zech. 2:10-12; 8:3).

The ark in 1 Kgs. 8:9 is of a fundamentally different nature. Here it is a container for the tablets of the Ten Commandments and a symbol of the covenant. The companion terminology is "ark of the covenant of the LORD" (vv. 1, 6). This understanding is especially associated with Deuteronomy (Deut. 10:5; 31:24-26). The association of the Decalogue with the ark is a way of saying that God's moral claim is at the heart of his being and is the essence of his presence. This conception of the ark was a needed corrective to the temptation to view God's presence as confined to the temple and as the guarantor of privilege.

The identification of these two voices enables us to discern a third, which knows God's presence to be elusive, numinous, and articulate. The symbolic and liturgical form of this experience of divine presence was the tent of meeting (1 Kgs. 8:4). God does not dwell in the tent but from time to time descends upon it in a cloud that represents his glory (vv. 10-11). Upon descending, God may make known his will. In the case of Moses, God spoke to him "face to face, as a man speaks to a friend" (Exod. 33:7-11; cf. Num. 11:16-17, 24-25; 12; Deut. 31:14-15).

These different voices bear testimony to the manifold aspects of God's presence and to the selectivity of human perception. Each voice is a witness to an authentic experience of divine presence as it was nurtured by a distinct group within Israel. The understanding of the ark as the throne of the living presence of God seems to have been the view that was most widely held. The conceptions of God's presence as moral claim (the Ten Commandments) and as glory (the cloud) have been included to supplement and correct it.

Solomon's Authorization for Building the Temple (8:14-21)

The next stage in the dedication is an address by Solomon to "all the assembly of Israel." It is presupposed that Solomon, standing before the altar (1 Kgs. 8:22, 55), faced the temple while delivering his dedicatory remarks (vv. 12-13). He then turns and faces those assembled in the courtyard (v. 14). Solomon blesses God for fulfilling Nathan's prophecy (v. 15), reviews this prophecy (vv. 16-19), and declares that his succession and building of the temple are the fulfillment of it (vv. 20-21).

For all the favor with which the temple came to be regarded, initially it was a disturbing innovation. For some two centuries previously God had sojourned variously at Gilgal, Shechem, Bethel, Shiloh, and Gibeon. To give up this free, itinerant existence for one exclusive place and to exchange a tent for a temple (2 Sam. 7:1-7) was a radical development. It is to these apprehensions that Solomon's remarks are addressed. He justifies his building of the temple by Nathan's prophecy (2 Sam. 7). In a free paraphrase of the prophet's words (esp. 2 Sam. 7:5-13), Solomon admits that God had not asked for a temple, but had approved David's desire to build one, yet deferred its actual building to David's son. Solomon declares that he is that son and therefore divinely authorized to build the temple. The construction of the temple is thus a development in accordance with God's will because it was initiated by David whom God had chosen and built by one whom God had promised.

The reference to the temple as the place of God's name (1 Kgs. 8:16, 17, 18, 19, 20) may strike one at first as a strange thought. But there is a mysterious power in a name, and it has a certain objective existence apart from the person it identifies. As we get to know a person, all his or her personality traits become concentrated in that person's name. Simply to utter it invokes one's presence and brings to life his or her personhood. (Note how a signature legally represents the one it designates.) God's name is God in his known, addressable nature, suggestive of a person of the Godhead. To say that God's name is present in the temple denotes his real presence but preserves the mystery of his transcendence. This conception of God's presence, which is especially associated with Deuteronomy (Deut. 12:5, 11, and often), is formulated to guard against understanding God's dwelling in the temple (1 Kgs. 8:13) to mean that he was confined to it.

Dedicatory Prayers (8:22-53)

The heart of ch. 8 is a series of prayers. They fall into two major categories: a prayer for the continual rule of David's sons upon the throne of Israel (vv. 22-26) and prayers for the temple as the spiritual link between God and Israel (vv. 27-53).

Prayer for Continual Rule over Israel (8:22-26)

8:22   *Place and Posture of Solomon.* Solomon stood "before the altar" with his hands uplifted to heaven. The custom of standing or kneeling in prayer varied (cf. v. 54), but uplifted hands seems to have been the uniform practice (vv. 38, 54; Exod. 9:22; Job 11:13; Isa. 1:15). 1 Kgs. 8:22 contains the first direct reference to the altar in chs. 6–8. Solomon is credited with building the altar in 9:25, but this may mean only that he remodeled or possibly converted to bronze (cf. 8:64; 2 Chr. 4:1) the altar David built on the threshing floor purchased from Araunah (2 Sam. 24:18-25).

8:23-24   *Praise of God's Incomparable Faithfulness.* Solomon first focuses his praise on that aspect of God's personality to which he wants to appeal, God's incomparability: "There is no God like thee, in heaven above or on earth beneath." Of the many examples of God's incomparability, Solomon singles out his "keeping covenant and showing steadfast love to thy servants who walk before thee with all their heart" (cf. Deut. 7:9, 12; 1 Kgs. 3:6). This trait is brought into sharp focus by reference to Nathan's prophecy to David that a son would succeed him and build a house for the LORD (2 Sam. 7:12-16). Solomon declares that his construction of the temple is the fulfillment of this prophecy and the proof of God's faithfulness (cf. 1 Kgs. 3:6).

8:25-26 *Solomon's Petition.* Solomon then asks God to confirm his promise to David that "There shall never fail you a man before me to sit upon the throne of Israel, if only your sons take heed to their way, to walk before me as you have walked before me." This promise is related to the covenant made with the northern tribes (2 Sam. 5:1-3; see the discussion of this covenant at 1 Kgs. 2:4).

Prayers concerning the Temple (8:27-51)

The purpose of these prayers is twofold: to consecrate the temple as a house of prayer and to define typical circumstances of prayer.

Consecration of the Temple as a House of Prayer (8:27-30)

Underlying this prayer is the theology of the ark as the receptacle of the tables of the Ten Commandments and the temple as the place of God's name (8:9, 16-21). As vv. 12-13 are the classic expression of the theology of the temple as the place of the indwelling presence of God, so vv. 27-30 are the fundamental statement of the theology of the temple as the place of God's name and a house of prayer.

Solomon introduces his prayer with the grand rhetorical question: "But will God indeed dwell on the earth?" (v. 27a). This question seems to be consciously formulated in relation to Solomon's statement in v. 13, "I have built thee an exalted house, a place for thee to dwell in for ever," and to anticipate or reflect the abuses to which this idea lends itself. The answer is a soaring affirmation of the transcendence of God who is beyond all confinement, even the heavens themselves: "Behold, heaven and the highest heaven cannot contain thee; how much less this house which I have built!" (v. 27b).

If God does not dwell in the temple, what then is its function? It is not empty. God's name is there. It is therefore a place of communication between God and mankind—somewhat like a communications satellite—the place par excellence where God responds to the invocation of his name, a house of prayer. Solomon petitions God, who dwells in heaven (vv. 30, 32, 34, 36, 39, 43, 45, 49), to be attentive "night and day" to the prayers of the king and people "when they pray toward this place." His prayer is in effect the consecration of the temple (parallel to that of vv. 12-13) as a house of prayer.

Seven Circumstances of Prayer (8:31-51)

Solomon next describes seven typical circumstances of need where the people in the future may seek God's help through the mediating agency of the temple. He petitions God to hear "in heaven . . . thy dwelling place" and to act favorably. Most of these circumstances are elaborated in some way, as by identifying their cause, specifying how the petition is to be made, or supplying the reason why God should respond favorably.

8:31-32 *First Circumstance: Juridical Oaths.* The situation anticipated here is a case where no witnesses or legal evidence is available and the issue is to be decided by an oath sworn by the accused before the altar (cf. Exod. 22:7-12; Num. 5:11-31). The oath is a potential curse that the accused calls down upon himself or herself if he or she swears falsely. The LORD is implored to work through this procedure so that justice prevails.

8:33-34 *Second Circumstance: Defeat in Battle.* It is assumed as self-evident that the basic cause of defeat is sin. By the same logic, the remedy for defeat is turning to God, acknowledging his name, praying, and making supplication to him. If and when such a response is made, God is requested to heed it and to "bring them again to the land which thou gavest to their fathers." The reference to exile is evidently a later amplification to take account of Israel's subsequent experiences of exile, as in 734, 722, 597. Whatever the vantage point of the one making this amplification, it is anticipated that those praying in the manner prescribed will do so "in this house," that is, in the courtyard of the temple (see above on 6:36). This excludes the exile of 587, when the temple was destroyed.

8:35-36 *Third Circumstance: Drought.* Drought, too, is understood as a punishment for sin. However, drought is not an end in itself but presents an opportunity for God to "teach them the good way in which they should walk." The remedy is prayer, acknowledgment of God's name, and penitence.

8:37-40 *Fourth Circumstance: Famine and Famine-producing Calamities.* The relation of these calamities to sin is also presupposed, for God is entreated both to hear and to forgive. Indeed, God's answer is contingent on the genuineness of one's repentance, on one's being smitten in conscience, for God knows the human heart. God should respond favorably so that the petitioner may "fear" (i.e., reverently acknowledge) the LORD as God.

8:41-43 *Fifth Circumstance: When the Foreigner Prays to the Lord.* This petition comes as a delightful surprise in the sequence. No attempt is made to anticipate the several reasons for the foreigner's prayer, and Solomon simply requests that God "do according to all for which the foreigner calls to thee." The reason the foreigner comes to pray at the temple is that he has heard of the LORD's great name. God is entreated to answer his prayer, "that all the peoples of the earth may know thy name and fear [revere] thee, as do thy people Israel." These verses prepare the way for the temple to become a house of prayer for all people (Isa. 56:6-7; Mark 11:17).

8:44-45 *Sixth Circumstance: Prayer for Victory in Battle.* The battle contemplated here is one into which God has sent his people in holy war. As in 1 Kgs. 8:33-34, victory is dependent, not on the size of the army, but on God's support of one's cause. The means for securing this is prayer toward Jerusalem, "the city which thou hast chosen," and the temple.

8:46-51 *Seventh Circumstance: Exile.* As in the case of defeat in battle, drought, and famine, so also exile is understood to be caused by sin. Again, the remedy is repentance, here spelled out as taking to heart and confessing one's sin, turning with all one's mind and heart to God, and praying toward the homeland, Jerusalem, and the temple (vv. 47-48; cf. Dan. 6:10; Jonah 2:4). The petition is for God to maintain the cause of exiled persons, to forgive them, and to "grant them compassion in the sight of those who carried them captive" (1 Kgs. 8:49-50). God should heed their prayers because they are his people, made so by his gracious act of liberation from the "iron furnace" of Egyptian bondage (v. 51; cf. Deut. 4:20; Jer. 11:4). The fact that the petition is for the compassion of their captors rather than return from exile (as in 1 Kgs. 8:34) suggests that it was added at a time when Israel was experiencing exile and there was no hope for an immediate return. The tone is similar to that of Jeremiah's letter to the exiles of 597 counselling them to accept exile for it would last seventy years (Jer. 29; cf. Ps. 106:46). Still, the reference to the liberation from Egyptian bondage (1 Kgs. 8:51) is a reminder that God is the one who delivers.

Concluding Appeal for God's Attentiveness (8:52-53)

As the seven circumstances of prayer are preceded (vv. 28-30), so they are followed by a prayer for God's attentiveness. God is petitioned that his eyes as well as his ears be open to the prayers made to him, that is, that he take into account the total person praying as well as the words of the prayer. God should be attentive to the prayers of king and people because at the time of liberation from Egyptian bondage he separated them from all the peoples of the earth to be his heritage (cf. Deut. 4:20; 9:29; Lev. 20:24, 26).

Blessing and Exhortation of the People (8:54-61)

8:54-55 *Solomon's Place and Posture.* Whereas 1 Kgs. 8:22 describes Solomon as standing while he prayed, here he is pictured as kneeling before the altar so that he must stand to bless those assembled. Both standing (Gen. 18:22; 1 Sam 1:26) and kneeling positions for prayer (1 Kgs. 19:18; 2 Kgs. 1:13; 2 Chr. 6:13; Ezra 9:5; Ps. 95:6; Isa. 45:23; Dan. 6:10; Acts 20:36) are mentioned in the OT. Has Solomon fallen to his knees in earnestness as he prayed? Or is 1 Kgs. 8:54 the imprint of a later generation reflecting its own practice in prayer?

8:56 *Thanksgiving for God's Faithfulness to His Promises.* Solomon first gives thanks to God for giving rest to Israel as he had promised. "Rest" *(menuhah)* is an expression for the security and well-being that mark the culmination of Israel's epic pilgrimage from a "wandering Aramean" to a free people in their own land with a proper place of worship. This has come about because of the power of God's promises working in and through the people. As Solomon thinks back over the history of Israel and recalls all the obstacles they had to overcome—Egyptian bondage, trials of the desert, threats from neighboring nations—he is filled with awe: "Not one word has failed of all his good promise, which he uttered by Moses his servant" (so also Josh. 21:45; 23:14). The power of God's promises in the past is also a source of confidence for the future.

8:57-60   *Solomon's Wishes.* Solomon's blessing now assumes the form of two wishes for himself and the people. The first is for God's continual presence that he may incline the hearts of the people to be obedient (1 Kgs. 8:57-58). Underlying this wish is the thought that Israel's highest good is God's presence, that this presence is contingent on obedience (6:11-13), and that it is God's grace that makes obedience possible. The second wish is that God may bear in mind Solomon's words day and night and maintain the cause of king and people "that all the peoples of the earth may know that the LORD is God; there is no other" (8:59-60). The maintenance of the "cause" (literally, "justice") of king and people has reference primarily to victory over adversaries (vv. 43, 49). The motivation for this wish is the concern that Israel's God may be triumphant over all obstacles and that Israel may fulfill their role as God's witness to the world.

8:61   *Concluding Exhortations.* Solomon concludes by exhorting the people to keep their hearts wholly true to God and to live according to his statutes and commandments. In order for God to be present with them they must make room for him in their hearts; in order for God to maintain their cause, it must be worthy.

The Festive Conclusion (8:62-66)

The procession of the ark to the temple and the words spoken by Solomon would have taken only a small amount of time. The major portion of the dedication consisted in sacrificial rites and ceremonies. Since the dedication coincided with the Feast of

Booths, here called "the feast" (*hehag,* v. 65; cf. v. 2), the celebrants would also have participated in the traditional rites of this festival which lasted for seven days. "All Israel" was present, "a great assembly, from the entrance of Hamath to the Brook of Egypt," the northernmost and southernmost boundaries of the kingdom. The sacrifices were so numerous that the bronze altar could not accommodate them and the middle of the courtyard (the huge stone now housed by the Dome of the Rock?) had to be consecrated and utilized.

The festive setting has an important bearing on the words spoken. All the senses and faculties were addressed through pageantry, song and dance (Ps. 42:4), eating and drinking, fellowship with one's neighbors, and a feeling of being joined in an unbroken chain of generations to the larger entity that was Israel. All these activities were set in the context of the ending of the old year and the beginning of the new, a time of promise and destiny. Thus the words spoken were enhanced by this context of celebration, joy, fellowship, and promise. Caught up in these events, the narrator spontaneously identifies with the celebrating throng "before the LORD our God" (1 Kgs. 8:65).

The dedication ends in a feeling of euphoria, with the people blessing the king and departing for their homes "joyful and glad of heart for all the goodness that the LORD had shown to David his servant and to Israel his people."

The Answer to Solomon's Dedicatory Prayers (9:1-9)

9:1-2 In an experience similar to that at Gibeon (3:4-15), God appears to Solomon for the second time in a dream-vision and responds to his prayers made during the dedication of the temple. There are no visual or circumstantial details, and Solomon receives God's answer silently.

9:3-5 *The Answer to Solomon's Petitions.* God assures Solomon that he has heard (i.e., favorably received; cf. 5:8) his prayer and supplication made at the dedication ceremony and responds affirmatively to the request for the temple to become a house of prayer (9:3). Declaring that he has "consecrated" (i.e., accepted and claimed) the temple, God pledges to put his name there "for ever" and promises that "my eyes [cf. 8:29, 52] and my heart will be there for all time"—a vivid way of expressing divine awareness and compassion for those praying. This passage obviously belongs with those that understand the temple as the place of God's name and as a house of prayer (8:27-53).

God's response to Solomon's petition for the sustained rule of the house of David upon the throne of Israel (i.e., the northern tribes; cf. 2:4; 8:25-26; 11:11) is simply to reiterate the promise made to David (9:4-5). God neither confirms nor denies it; it is a promise whose actualization depends on the fulfillment of the conditions.

9:6-9 *A Warning of the Consequences of Disloyalty and Disobedience.* The "you" of v. 6 is plural in the Hebrew, and the address is to Solomon's successors. Solomon's prayers having been answered, God now speaks in warning of the dire consequences to the nation if Solomon's sons turn aside from following God and do not keep his commandments and statutes. The most damaging offense is to "go and serve other gods and worship them" (v. 6). So serious is this violation of the First Commandment that the consequences will be exile and the destruction of the temple, disasters of such magnitude as to excite the wonder of the world. But even to non-Israelites the reason will be obvious: "Because they [the people, by acquiescing, share in the king's guilt] forsook the LORD their God who brought their fathers out of the land of Egypt, and laid hold on other gods" (v. 9). Foreigners will also understand that it happened, not by default on the part of God, but that God himself "has brought all this evil upon them" (vv. 8, 9; cf. Deut. 28:36-37; 29:24-29; Jer. 22:8-9; 24:9).

THEOLOGICAL REFLECTIONS ON 8:1–9:9

As Moses states in Exod. 33:16, it is God's presence with Israel that is the basis of their distinctiveness. The most important expression of the reality of God's presence in ancient Israel was the temple. It was a reality grasped in three aspects: a dwelling presence, an elusive presence whose tangible manifestation is glory, and a name presence designating the transcendent but addressable nature of God who requires right conduct.

The theology of the dwelling presence of God gave rise to a wonderful sense of God's nearness and living reality. Nurtured by this understanding, the worshipper thirsted for the living God (Ps. 42:2) and came to Jerusalem to "seek the face of the God of Jacob" (Ps. 24:6; cf. 63:1), confident that "the God of gods will be seen in Zion" (Ps. 84:7). It was unbearable to be cut off from this presence (Pss. 42–43). A day there was better than a thousand elsewhere (Ps. 84:10). The highest good imaginable would be to dwell in the house (court) of the LORD forever (Ps. 23:6; 27:4; cf. 61:4). So real was God's presence in the temple that prophets spoke of God uttering his voice from Zion (Amos 1:2), while psalmists prayed to God to send help from the sanctuary to the king (Ps. 20:2) and faced threats to Jerusalem in the confidence that because of the presence of the LORD of hosts the city would be secure (e.g., Ps. 46).

This was also a theology that was easily perverted into a static conception of God's presence and feelings of false privilege and exclusiveness. The understanding of God's dwelling presence had become so distorted in the time of Jeremiah that he had to announce the destruction of the temple (Jer. 7:1-15; 26:1-15). The theology of name presence was an important corrective, but it did not save the temple, and in 587 Jeremiah's prophecy was fulfilled.

The absence of the ark and the temple was not a problem for some (cf. Jer. 3:15-18; Isa. 57:15; 66:1), but for most a tangible place of God's presence was important and a second temple was built between 520-515. But the cycle repeated itself, and in A.D. 70 this temple also was destroyed. By this time, however, the ultimate meaning of God's presence had been revealed in "something greater than the temple" (Matt. 12:6). Jesus is quoted as saying in the Gospel according to John, "Destroy this temple, and in three days I will raise it up." This saying is explained as meaning that "he spoke of the temple of his body" (John 2:19-21; Mark 14:58). At the time of his death "the curtain of the temple [before the inner sanctuary] was torn in two, from top to bottom" (Mark 15:38) and the mystery of the holy of holies was fully disclosed. The temple then is an important chapter in the theology of the Incarnation.

While the temple is the place of communion, praise, thanksgiving, confidence, and trust, 1 Kgs. 8 concentrates on its role in situations of distress. One is invited to petition God in any circumstance of need, but with the awareness that petition means more than a declaration of need and a plea for help. For petition to be effective, one must look for God's chastening hand in adversity, confess one's sins—confess with the knowledge that God knows the heart and is attentive with his "eyes" as well as his "ears"—and turn to God (repent) earnestly, sincerely, with one's whole heart.

Remarkably, sacrifice is not mentioned. Nor is one required to be physically present at the temple in order to approach God. It is effective to pray in the direction of the temple.

The account of the construction and dedication of the temple is framed by two sober warnings (6:11-13; 9:6-9). God graciously makes himself present in the temple and pledges to hear prayer attentively and compassionately. But God also states the conditions of his presence and blessings and warns of the consequences of disloyalty and disobedience. Juxtaposed to the elaborate and loving account of the building and dedication of the temple is the prospect of the absence of God's presence and even the destruction of the temple and the exile of the people! These possibilities are a reminder that the temple exists, not as a guarantee of security and endurance, but to facilitate communion with God and obedience to his will.

SOLOMON'S OTHER BUILDING ACTIVITIES (9:10-25)

Solomon's building activities are divided into two phases: the construction of the temple-palace complex and the construction of fortifications, chariot, and store-cities (9:10-23). The accounts of these two phases have been developed in parallelism to each other. Both accounts have in common an agreement with Hiram (5:1-2; 9:10-14), a description of Solomon's forced labor (5:13-18; 9:15a, 20-23), a list of building accomplishments (chs. 6–7; 9:15b-19), and both end with Solomon officiating as high priest (ch. 8; 9:25). The brevity of the account of the military projects is a measure of their importance relative to the temple-palace complex.

Solomon's Sale of Twenty Galilean Cities to Hiram of Tyre (9:10-14)

It is noteworthy that Solomon for all his might gave up rather than added to Israelite territory. His sale of twenty Galilean cities to

King Hiram of Tyre was obviously a regrettable loss (cf. 2 Chr. 8:1-2), but the point of the story is that Solomon got far more than he gave. The cities in question, located on the border of Hiram's kingdom, were "Cabul" ("good-for-nothing," Moffatt), as Hiram found out to his displeasure upon inspecting them. One hundred and twenty talents of gold, on the other hand, are more than four metric tons! No reason is given for Solomon's need of gold. Was the sale of these cities a desperate measure necessitated by the exhaustion of the Israelite treasury? Or was it a shrewd business deal to finance additional building projects?

Solomon's Forced Labor (9:15a, 20-23)

As with the temple-palace complex, so Solomon's other building projects were made possible by forced labor. Contrary to 1 Kgs. 5:13-18 (cf. 11:28), it is here maintained that the labor force was composed entirely of the remnant of the Canaanite population, with Israelites serving only as officers and making up the military. The difference between the two passages may be accounted for by the fact that the residue of Canaanites were made into a permanent "forced levy of slaves" (9:21), whereas Israelites were obliged to serve only on a limited and temporary basis as "a levy of forced labor" (5:13). The distinction is approximately that between serfdom and civic duty.

The subjection of the remnant of the Canaanites is to be understood in the light of Deut. 7:1-5; 20:10-18. According to these passages, Moses charged Israel to destroy utterly the native population of Canaan if they resisted Israel's efforts to settle the land. If the Canaanites made peace, Israel was to subject them to forced labor, "that they may not teach you to do according to all their abominable practices which they have done in the service of their gods" (Deut. 20:18; cf. Gen. 9:25-27; Josh. 23:12-13; 2 Kgs. 17:7-18). The Christian may be instructed by Deuteronomic realism not to be naive about the "Canaanites" of the present, but both the OT (e.g., Gen. 12:1-3; Exod. 23:4-5, 9; Isa. 19:23-25; 45:20-25; Amos 9:7; Jonah) and especially the NT (e.g., Matt. 5:43-48; Luke 6:27-36; Rom. 11:28; 12:20) have another theology with regard to the enemies of the covenant people that one will want to take into consideration.

Solomon's Military Construction Projects (9:15b-19)

This passage catalogues an impressive list of constructions: the Millo, the wall of Jerusalem, Hazor, Megiddo, Gezer, Lower Beth-horon, Baalath, and Tamar in the wilderness, "and whatever Solomon desired to build in Jerusalem, in Lebanon, and in all the land of his dominion" (1 Kgs. 9:19).

These projects reveal a concern to strengthen the kingdom militarily. The construction of the Millo (literally, "Filling") most likely refers to the building up and broadening of the narrow ridge between the old city of David and the new site of the temple and palace area (cf. 2 Sam. 5:9). The fact that this project is linked to the building of the wall of Jerusalem (probably around the new part of the city opened up by Solomon) shows that it was important to the defense of the city (1 Kgs. 11:27). Hazor was the most important city near Solomon's northern border and controlled the principal highway between Egypt and Mesopotamia. Megiddo commanded the most strategic pass on the coastal highway. Gezer and Lower Beth-horon were situated on the chief access routes to Jerusalem from the coastal plain. Baalath and Tamar in the wilderness are not known with certainty but apparently were strategically placed on Judah's southern flank. The store-cities and cities for chariots and horses (9:19) further confirm the military character of the projects listed above.

Solomon's military preparations may have been related to deteriorating relations with Egypt. The alliance established by the marriage to Pharaoh's daughter (3:1) did not last. An unnamed pharaoh gave aid and comfort to Solomon's adversary, Hadad the Edomite (11:14-22). Shishak, founder of the 22nd Dynasty (ca. 934), gave asylum to Jeroboam, who had "lifted up his hand against" Solomon (11:26-40), and shortly after Solomon's death Shishak invaded Palestine (14:25-26; 2 Chr. 12:1-9). Shishak's behavior confirms the importance of having Egypt as an ally and helps to explain Solomon's motives for marrying an Egyptian princess at the outset of his reign.

For all his military preparations, Solomon waged no war of conquest. Nor was his kingdom an impregnable fortress. When Shishak invaded Palestine he was able to move with ease through the land, and Solomon's successors, Rehoboam and Jeroboam, had to busy themselves with building fortifications (1 Kgs. 12:25; 2 Chr. 11:5-10).

Completion of the New Palace for Pharaoh's Daughter and Construction of the Millo (9:24)

Apparently the intention of this note is to record a chronological relationship, namely, that the palace of Pharaoh's daughter was the last building to be completed in the temple-palace complex (cf. 1 Kgs. 3:1) and the Millo was the first undertaking of the projects listed in 9:15b-19. The entry into (3:1) and exit of Pharaoh's daughter from the city of David also provides a time frame and rhetorical unity to the most important phase of Solomon's building activities.

Solomon Officiates at the Three Major Festivals (9:25)

This note hearkens back to the time when Solomon and the people worshipped at the high places (3:2, 3) and sums up the profound transformation in worship wrought by Solomon. It was the celebration of the cycle of the three major festivals that "finished" the temple, that is, fulfilled the purpose for which it was built. Solomon officiates at the three major festivals because in ancient Israel the king was a religious as well as a political leader. The king was God's son by adoption (Ps. 2:7), a priest after the order of Melchizedek (Ps. 110:4), and his chief responsibilities were to defend the powerless and to maintain justice, righteousness, and peace (e.g., Ps. 72; Isa. 9:7; 11:2-5). It was this ideal of kingship that led to the concept of the Messiah.

SOLOMON THE TRADER

1 Kings 9:26–10:29

Solomon's building activities are mentioned no more, and the next major unit of material (9:26–10:29) focuses on his trading enterprises and the legendary wealth and fame they brought him. Solomon's commercial enterprises were carried out on an international scale and with the same energy as the building projects. Wisdom continues to be understood as the basis of Solomon's success and attraction.

SOLOMON'S RED SEA FLEET (9:26-28)

This matter-of-fact account discloses a daring initiative in international trade. Although Israel borders the Mediterranean Sea, no seaworthy harbor was developed in OT times. The one port available to Solomon was at Ezion-geber in Edomite territory at the head of the Gulf of Aqaba, the tongue of the Red Sea east of the Sinai Peninsula. Taking advantage of his control of Edom, Solomon developed a merchant fleet for Israel. Inexperienced in shipbuilding and sailing, he again turned to Hiram and with Phoenician help built and manned a fleet harbored at Ezion-geber. Solomon's Red Sea fleet was a bold move to free Israel from the Arabian monopoly on trade with the southeastern portion of the biblical world. From Ezion-geber Solomon's fleet could ply the waters of the Red Sea, the Persian Gulf, and the Indian Ocean and go directly to the sources of supply. The most notable port of call, famous for its gold, was Ophir (1 Kgs. 22:48; Job 28:16; Ps. 45:9; Isa. 13:12). The association of Ophir with Sheba and Havilah in Gen. 10:28-29 points to a location in southwestern Arabia (Gen. 10:30) or Somaliland. From Ophir, gold "to the amount of four hundred and twenty talents" was brought to Solomon, proof of the resounding success of this enterprise.

THE VISIT OF THE QUEEN OF SHEBA (10:1-10, 13)

This colorful story shines brightly in the midst of a drab literary landscape of facts and statistics of trade and wealth. Many dignitaries and heads of state visited Solomon (1 Kgs. 4:34; 10:23-25), but none made such an impression or so excited the imagination as the queen of Sheba. The story is told to illustrate how impressive were Solomon's wisdom and wealth and how his fame compelled a female head of state from a distant land to visit him and bring him gifts. But the adventurous spirit, generosity, and adroitness of the queen of Sheba so captivate the narrator that it is she who dominates the account while Solomon appears passive and colorless. We do not know her by name, but the queen of Sheba is clearly one of the most interesting and charming personalities of the OT.

Sheba was located at the southwestern corner of the Arabian Peninsula, roughly equivalent to modern Yemen, about 2,250 km. (1,400 mi.) from Jerusalem. Apparently Sheba was a dual kingdom that included Seba (a variant spelling of Sheba) on the African mainland (cf. Ps. 72:10). The Red Sea, only 24 km. (15 mi.) wide at Bab el-Mandeb, provides easy access between Arabia and Africa. If Sheba-Seba was a single kingdom politically, its ethnic composition was diverse. The people of Sheba are credited with both a Semitic and Hamitic ancestry, suggesting a mixed population. In Gen. 10:28; 25:3; and 1 Chr. 1:32 Sheba's lineage is traced to Shem, but in Gen. 10:7 it is linked to Ham. Seba, however, is related only to Ham (Gen. 10:7; 1 Chr. 1:9) and is clearly African (Isa. 43:3; 45:14; cf. Cain Hope Felder, *Troubling Biblical Waters*, ch. 2).

The early history of Sheba is not well known, but in the time of Solomon it appears to have been the strongest and most prosperous kingdom in southwestern Arabia and northeastern Africa. The basis of its prosperity and strength was trade. Sheba was the chief supplier of frankincense, one of the most desirable products in the biblical world, and was also famous for gold and precious gems (Ps. 72:15; Isa. 60:6; Jer. 6:20; Ezek. 27:22; 38:13). Moreover, Sheba was located in a strategic position relative to world markets. Situated at the confluence of the Red Sea and Indian Ocean, Sheba had access by sea to the east coast of Africa

and to India. By land Sheba was linked with the great caravan
route that ran along the eastern shore of the Red Sea to Teima
(Job 6:19) and from thence to Mesopotamia, Egypt, and Europe.
Sovereign of a kingdom that was a major force in international
trade, the queen who visited Solomon was impressive in her own
right.

It was not unusual for a woman to be head of state in this part
of the world. Five different queens from north Arabia are mentioned in Assyrian inscriptions from the 8th and 7th cents. B.C.
(cf. Acts 8:27). Some even led troops in combat (cf. Nabia Abbott,
"Pre-Islamic Arab Queens").

10:1-3 *The Queen's Arrival and the Contest with Solomon.* Solomon's fleet in the Red Sea (1 Kgs. 9:26-28; 10:22) would
inevitably have come in contact with Sheba. In this way the queen
would have heard of the Israelite king and his God. According to
v. 1, she came out of the love of wisdom that she shared with
Solomon. The two also had in common rival commercial interests.

The caravan route from Sheba came under Solomon's control
at the head of the gulf of Aqaba. On the other hand, Solomon's
Red Sea fleet was an encroachment on Sheba's sphere of influence.
It is very likely, therefore, that Solomon and the queen discussed
commercial matters as well as wisdom. Israel's trading venture on
the Red Sea was soon abandoned (22:48), the political and
commercial negotiations forgotten, but the visit of the queen and
her personality are fondly remembered.

Wisdom was highly prized throughout the biblical world,
especially in court circles, and contests between heads of state were
a traditional part of court etiquette. It was quite in order, then,
for the queen of Sheba to test Solomon with "hard questions"
(*hidot;* cf. Judg. 14:12-14). In this particular contest, Solomon
was the decisive winner. There was no question he could not
answer, nothing he could not explain.

10:4-5 *The Queen's Impression of Solomon and His World.* The
queen's reason for visiting Solomon, her arrival, and the contest
(1 Kgs. 10:1-3) are narrated succinctly and dryly, but her response
following the besting by Solomon is recounted vividly and in
detail. Those things that impressed her were: Solomon's wisdom,

the house he had built (probably his palace), the food on his table, the seating of his officials, the attendance of his servants, their clothing, his cupbearers, and the burnt offerings he sacrificed at the temple. This list suggests that the contest (and trade negotiations) was part of an elaborate agenda that included a state dinner and worship at the temple. The queen's domestic interests are given prominence here, but her real concerns, as the following verses reveal, were with affairs of state. So great was her amazement and admiration that "there was no more spirit in her"; she was overwhelmed.

10:6-9 *The Queen's Speech in Praise of Solomon.* The queen's nonverbal response is followed by a generous, eloquent speech of concession. It was a mark of wisdom to be able to speak well, and in this the queen excels. She begins by stating that the report she had heard of Solomon's affairs and wisdom, while true as far as it went, was inadequate. "Behold," she exclaims, "the half of it was not told me!" In particular, she congratulates Solomon on the happiness of his wives (fittingly spoken by a woman, but inappropriate for a man) and his servants, not because of the magnificence of their clothing (which she did appreciate, v. 5), but because they were privileged to be continually in Solomon's presence and to hear his wisdom. Finally, she touches on Solomon's kingship. Perceiving in his achievements the evidence that he had been divinely chosen, she places the final seal of approval on Solomon's succession: "Blessed be the LORD your God, who has delighted in you and set you on the throne of Israel! Because the LORD loved Israel for ever, he has made you king. . . ." The reader familiar with Nathan's prophecy in 2 Sam. 7 would recognize the queen's words as another inadvertent confirmation that Solomon's succession was the fulfillment of that prophecy (cf. 1 Kgs. 5:7). The queen understands well the essence of the kingly office and the purpose for which Solomon had been chosen, namely to "execute justice and righteousness" (10:9).

The different meanings of wisdom encountered in 3:4-15 and 4:29-33 mingle together in this passage. In 10:1-3, 8 wisdom is intellectual astuteness, learning, and insight gained from observation of nature (cf. 4:29-33). In 10:4-7 wisdom is a divine gift that makes for good government and prosperity (cf. 3:4-15, 16-28; ch. 4).

10:10, 13   *Gift Giving and the Queen's Departure.* At the conclusion of her visit the queen gave Solomon 120 talents of gold (the same sum Hiram gave for twenty cities!), precious stones, and "a very great quantity of spices," the likes of which had never been seen before or since in Jerusalem (10:10). Solomon's gifts are not named, but he gave generously and added to his initial offerings whatever the queen desired or requested (v. 13a). Hidden behind this language is undoubtedly an agreement concerning mutual trade interests. After the gift giving the queen returned home (v. 13b).

All the OT has to say about the queen of Sheba is contained in 1 Kgs. 10:1-10, 13 and the parallel passage in 2 Chr. 9:1-9, 12, but she lives on in legend. Her visit and especially the statements that "she came to [or 'came in to'] Solomon" (v. 2) and that Solomon gave her "all that she desired," interpreted romantically, have engendered a rich body of literature among Jews, Arabs, and Ethiopians (for a survey and summary of this literature, cf. William L. Hansberry, "The Queen of Sheba"). Her visit is also a popular theme in Christian art and literature. Because of the dual nature of the kingdom of Sheba-Seba, both Arabs and Ethiopians claim the queen as their own. Josephus refers to her as the "queen of Egypt and Ethiopia" (*Ant.* viii.6.2, 5-6), and in the NT she is called "the queen of the South" (Matt. 12:42; Luke 11:31; cf. also Origen *Commentarius in Canticum Cantorum* ii.367-370; Jerome *De Actibus Apostolorum* i.673-707, cited by F. M. Snowden, Jr., *Blacks in Antiquity,* 202-4). Ethiopians have given the queen's visit a prominent place in their classic national chronicle, *Kebra Nagast (Glory of the Kings).* According to this saga a son, Menelik, was born to the queen as a result of the visit, and the claim was written into the Revised Constitution of 1955 that the royal line of Emperor Haile Selassie "descends without interruption from the dynasty of Menelik I son of the Queen of Ethiopia, the Queen of Sheba, and King Solomon of Jerusalem" (Article II).

10:11-12   *A Note on Trade with Ophir.* This note has been added to the story of the queen of Sheba possibly because trade with Ophir was a principal result of the queen's visit. Of the cargo from Ophir, almug timbers (*'atse almuggim,* an obscure term apparently designating a hard, reddish sandalwood) and its great quantity are of chief interest to the annotator. That it was restricted in use to the temple, the king's palace, and for making musical instruments shows how highly prized it was.

SOLOMON'S WEALTH, WISDOM, AND POWER (10:14-29)

10:14-15 *Solomon's Annual Income in Gold.* The total of 666 talents of gold (1 Kgs. 10:14) seems to be computed on the basis of the 120 talents received from Hiram (9:14), the 120 talents from the queen of Sheba (10:10), and the 420 talents from Ophir (9:28) and to represent a peak year of income rather than a typical year (with 6 talents from an unnamed source).

1 Kgs. 10:15 names the principal sources of revenue from taxation: traders, merchants, all the kings of Arabia, and the governors of the land. The distinction between "traders" and "merchants" is apparently between those using Israelite trade routes in international commerce and those doing business with Israel. The "kings of Arabia" were rulers in north Arabia who traded with Israel or transported their goods through Israelite territory. "Governors of the land" were probably the tax administrators of 4:7-19, although they are designated by a different word (*pahot* rather than *nitstsabim*). According to James A. Montgomery, "The reference to taxation of international merchandising is of interest as probably the earliest record of the kind that we possess" (*The Books of Kings*, 220).

10:16-17 *Solomon's Golden Shields.* From the vast amount of gold available to him, Solomon made two hundred large and three hundred small shields. The narrator is not concerned with their shape, design, or purpose, but with the plentiful supply and generous use of gold they represent. Six hundred shekels (about 10 kilograms or 22 lbs. avoirdupois weight) were used for the large shields and three minas (about 3 kilograms or 6.6 lbs. avoirdupois) for the small ones. The gold was "beaten," that is, overlaid on a base of wood or metal. The shields were stored in the House of the Forest of Lebanon and were used by the royal bodyguard who accompanied the king whenever he "went into the house of the LORD" (14:28).

10:18-20 *Solomon's Gold and Ivory Throne.* This is one of the best described of all Solomon's works. It is not that the entire throne was made of ivory, but that a wooden framework was so generously inlaid with ivory and plated with gold that the woodwork was scarcely if at all visible. Six steps led to the seat of the throne. An interesting question, but one impossible to answer, is whether the throne and its decorations were intended to be symbolic or not. According to popular thought the universe was divided into seven levels. Did the throne symbolize the cosmos so that the king, enthroned on the highest level, formed the divinely ordained link between God and creation, or was this simply the traditional way to make a throne? Were the calf's head at the back of the throne, the two lions standing beside the arm rests, and the lion at each end of the six steps symbolic (cf. Gen. 49:9), or were they merely traditional decorative motifs?

10:21 *The Drinking Vessels of Gold.* So abundant was gold—"it was not considered as anything in the days of Solomon"—that all his drinking vessels and "all the vessels of the House of the Forest of Lebanon" were made of it.

10:22 *Revenue from the Red Sea Fleet.* This is the third reference to this fleet (1 Kgs. 9:26-28; 10:11; cf. 22:48) and adds some important details. The ships are characterized as "ships of Tarshish," a term designating large, oceangoing vessels. Hiram also had a fleet in the Red Sea (9:27; 10:11), and the two fleets operated together. The ships went to sea for three years at a time, and their cargoes consisted of gold, silver, ivory, apes, and peacocks (or baboons; cf. RSV mg, NEB, NIV). The size of the ships, the length of time at sea, and the cargo suggest voyages to the east coast of Africa and to India.

10:23-25 *Gifts and Homage from Abroad.* So great were Solomon's riches and wisdom that they won for him hegemony over the hearts of all his contemporaries. "The whole earth" sought him out to hear his wisdom, "which God had put into his mind" (v. 24), and to bring him gifts (*minhah* also means "tribute") of silver and gold, garments, myrrh, spices, horses, and mules. The passage is akin to Ps. 72, where worldwide homage is claimed for the king of

Israel because he is the chosen and anointed one of God and the chief agent of his purposes on earth. 1 Kgs. 10:23-25 lacks, however, the emphasis on the maintenance of justice and righteousness and the protection of the poor and weak found in the psalm.

10:26-29   *Solomon's Chariot Force.* Wealth makes for power, and in the biblical world chariots were an important symbol of a nation's might. In this respect Solomon also excelled, having fourteen hundred chariots and twelve thousand horses (cf. 4:26). The great expense of maintaining this force is implied by the reference to Solomon's making silver as common as stone in Jerusalem and cedar as plentiful as sycamore (10:27). Verses 28-29 give factual but obscure information about where Solomon purchased chariots and horses (cf. JB, NIV, TEV), the price of each, and an ambiguous note about international trade in chariots and horses. The role of Israelite merchants in this trade is not as clear as the translation of RSV suggests (cf. NEB).

THEOLOGICAL REFLECTIONS ON 9:26–10:29

On the basis of 9:26–10:29 it is clear that Solomon was determined to achieve prosperity, splendor, and security. To do so, he exploited every possible source of wealth. His initiative and boldness, as in the Red Sea venture, are impressive. No means of revenue escaped his attention. Material well-being is not frowned on in the Bible. What is condemned is covetousness, wealth acquired unjustly, self-indulgence, and anxious preoccupation with material things (Exod. 20:17; Amos 6:1-7; Matt. 6:24-33; Luke 12:13-21).

The positive effects of the prosperity, splendor, and security Solomon achieved are pictured in 1 Kgs. 4:20-21, 24-25. It is clear from chs. 11 and 12, however, that these achievements were paid for with a high price in human oppression. The drinking vessels of gold, the golden shields, and the lavish use of silver and cedar were extravagant. Armaments are expensive then as now and squander a nation's resources. And a king, according to Deut. 17:16-17, should not multiply horses nor silver and gold for himself.

The story of the visit of the queen of Sheba, while intended to glorify Solomon, mirrors one of the finest portraits of a woman in the OT. The queen is admired, but her office and ability are not regarded as something exceptional because she was a woman. Nor is she treated in a patronizing or condescending manner. It is a tribute to the maturity of the editors of 1 Kings that the finest human tribute to Solomon comes from a foreigner who also happened to be a woman.

There is no indication that the queen was converted to Solomon's religion. Yet she serves as a type of those who are attracted to God's covenant people. Her effort and enthusiasm shame those who have One greater than Solomon (Matt. 12:42; Luke 11:31) but all too often do not regard getting to know him as a journey worth taking.

SOLOMON THE SINNER
1 Kings 11:1-43

The account of Solomon's reign in 1 Kgs. 3–10 is a record of ever increasing success and fame. But instead of coming to a restful and satisfying end, the story of Solomon concludes on a dissonant note. The kingdom, built up so impressively, is destined for dissolution. This development comes so abruptly that ch. 11 stands in tension with what has preceded. Now it is revealed that there has been long-standing opposition to Solomon in Edom and Syria and that the discontent of the northern tribes was such that they needed only a leader to revolt.

SOLOMON'S SIN (11:1-13)

11:1-8 *Solomon's Many Foreign Wives and His Apostasy.* As Solomon's building program, wealth, and fame were on a grand scale, so was his harem. Seven hundred wives and three hundred concubines are not unprecedented, but never before or after did an Israelite king have so many wives. The next largest harem was Rehoboam's eighteen wives and sixty concubines (2 Chr. 11:21). David had at least eight wives (2 Sam. 3:2-5; 5:13-16; 11:27; 1 Chr. 3:1-9) and some ten or more concubines (2 Sam. 15:16). Only one of David's wives is known to have been a foreigner (2 Sam. 13:37; 1 Chr. 3:2).

The text does not disapprove of the large number of Solomon's wives and concubines directly. Many marriages were proof of a ruler's virility and evidence of a powerful life force to facilitate his rule (but cf. Deut. 17:17). What is objected to is Solomon's clinging in love to foreign women whom Israelites were forbidden to marry (1 Kgs. 11:1, 2). Such a prohibition is found in Deut. 7:1-5 (cf. Exod. 34:15-16; Josh. 23:12-13) and is one of the many indications of the influence of Deuteronomy on the narrator of this passage. The reason for this objection is not racial but religious.

Solomon's marriages were a means to further political goals (1 Kgs. 3:1). By marrying the daughter of a local clan chieftain or potentate in one of his subject countries or allies, Solomon secured goodwill, loyalty, and peace. But marriage to foreign women also opened the way to Solomon's heart being turned after their gods (11:2, 4), thus violating the First Commandment. He who at the beginning of his reign was noted for his love of God (3:3), at the end is famous for his love of women. That Solomon clung in love to his foreign wives suggests that his character was flawed by an inordinate desire for women.

There are mitigating circumstances to Solomon's sin, but he is held fully responsible. On the one hand, Solomon's turning away from the LORD is blamed on his wives (11:3, 4) and dated to his old age (v. 4). On the other hand, Solomon is regarded as accountable and his turning away is depicted as a gradual, subtle yielding that culminated near the end of his reign. Solomon begins by loving many foreign women and clinging to them in love (vv. 1-3). Next, he becomes accepting of other gods; "his heart was not wholly true," and he did not "wholly follow" the LORD (vv. 4, 5, 6). Consequently, he "went after" Ashtoreth, the fertility goddess of the Sidonians, and Milcom, the national god of the Ammonites (v. 5). Then he built a high place on "the mountain east of Jerusalem" (the Mount of Olives) for Chemosh, the national god of Moab, and for Molech (a title of Milcom, v. 7). Finally, yielding fully, "so he did for all his foreign wives" (v. 8).

11:9-13 *The Judgment.* Verses 1-8 summarize a long and complex drift into apostasy, but it is not until near the end of Solomon's reign that he becomes liable for judgment. The judgment is announced by the narrator, who makes us privy to God's feelings about Solomon (vv. 9-10) and lets us hear the judgment as coming directly from God (vv. 11-13).

God was angry with Solomon because "his heart had turned away," and this in spite of the fact that God had appeared to him twice (3:4-15; 9:1-9) and warned him about going after other gods (11:9-10). The announcement of judgment falls, typically, into two parts: the reason for the judgment and the judgment itself. The reason for the judgment is that "this has been your mind and you have not kept my covenant and my statutes which I have commanded you" (v. 11). "This has been your mind" means that despite any mitigating circumstances (vv. 3-4) Solomon is fully responsible for his behavior. The phrase even suggests deliberate intent (cf. Job 10:13 and TEV). "My covenant and my statutes" must refer, as in 1 Kgs. 2:4; 8:25-26; 9:4-5, to the covenant between David and the northern tribes mentioned in 2 Sam. 5:1-3 (see the discussion on 2:4 above).

The judgment is that God will tear the kingdom from Solomon and give it to one of his servants (subordinate officials), the same penalty as in the other references to the covenant with the northern tribes. But the judgment is tempered with grace. The rending of the kingdom is postponed to the reign of Solomon's son (1 Kgs. 11:12), and not all the kingdom will be torn away. God will give Solomon's son one tribe (either Judah, 12:20; 2 Kgs. 17:18, or Benjamin in addition to Judah, 1 Kgs. 12:21, 23; the ambiguity exists because Benjamin was divided between the northern and southern kingdoms and could be reckoned to either). The mitigation of the judgment is not because of anything Solomon does but "for the sake of David my servant and for the sake of Jerusalem which I have chosen" (1 Kgs. 11:13b). Underlying God's grace is the covenant with David (2 Sam. 7) and the choice of Jerusalem as the LORD's cultic home (2 Sam. 6; 1 Kgs. 8).

THEOLOGICAL REFLECTIONS ON 11:1-13

The basic reason for the undoing of Solomon's kingdom was Solomon's violation of the First Commandment (11:1-10). The First Commandment is here thought of in its positive as well as its negative formulations, and Solomon violated both. His heart was not "wholly true" (v. 4). He did not "wholly follow" (v. 6) or love the LORD with all his heart, with all his soul, and with all his might (Deut. 6:5). Solomon also broke the First Commandment in its negative form (Exod. 20:3; Deut. 5:7). His heart was turned away (1 Kgs. 11:4; cf. v. 3), and he "went after" other gods (v. 5). The text does not say that he actually worshipped other gods. "Went after" is defined by the context as permissive tolerance of other gods and support of their worship. By linking the disruption of the kingdom to Solomon's violation of the First Commandment, the narrator affirms that this commandment is critical to human life and destiny.

This passage is instructive as to the true source of the security of a people. Through his many marriages Solomon sought to strengthen his realm by cultivating good relations within his kingdom and with neighboring states. He was not as concerned to maintain a good relationship with God. Solomon assumed that the chief threat to him was the anger of some political enemy. The real threat to him was the anger of God. Solomon's true security lay in regarding the LORD as holy and making the LORD the object of his fear and dread (Isa. 8:13).

Outwardly all was fair in Solomon's kingdom for most of his reign, but all along sin was at work like a cancerous growth and suddenly burst forth in all its ugly, destructive force. Sin begins like a tiny crack in a high wall and spreads until the whole wall is weakened and suddenly collapses with a mighty crash (Isa. 30:13-14). God responds to Solomon's sin with anger, an anger that developed over the long course of Solomon's slide into apostasy, for God is slow to anger (Exod. 34:6-7). God becomes angry because he is not neutral or indifferent to human behavior. God passionately cares and takes sin seriously. But anger is not the last word with God, nor does he permit sin to defeat his purposes.

Two covenant traditions stand side by side in the announcement of judgment on Solomon: the conditional covenant with the northern tribes (1 Kgs. 2:4; 8:25; 9:4-5) and the unconditional covenant with David (2 Sam. 7). The conditional covenant with the northern tribes has to do with political control; the unconditional covenant with David is bound up with God's ultimate purposes in the world. Political control is not vital to the covenant people and is contingent on obedience. The Davidic dynasty and Jerusalem, however, were crucial to God's purposes, and God is steadfast in his commitment to them (cf. 1 Kgs. 11:36; 5:4; 2 Kgs. 8:19). When a descendant of David commits iniquity, God chastens him with the "rod of men" but does not reject him (2 Sam. 7:14b-15; 1 Kgs. 11:39). God remained steadfast in his commitment to David even when Judah ceased to be a political state in 587 B.C., and in the fullness of time brought forth a "lamp" (*nir*; cf. 2 Sam. 14:7; 21:17; 1 Kgs. 11:36; 15:4; 2 Kgs. 8:19; Ps. 132:17) who became the light of the world (John 1:4-9; 8:12; 9:5).

THREE ADVERSARIES OF SOLOMON (11:14-40)

These verses show how the judgment announced against Solomon in 1 Kgs. 11:11-13 was fulfilled. Three adversaries—Hadad the Edomite, Rezon the Syrian, and Jeroboam the Ephraimite—rise against Solomon and become the agents for the dissolution of his kingdom. On the surface the causal relationship between sin and judgment seems forced. The opposition of each adversary was carried on independently of the others, and each was motivated by a different reason. Moreover, each opponent was active over an extended period and not just at the end of Solomon's reign when the judgment was announced. The opposition of Solomon's adversaries, however, was not by chance. God "raised up" Hadad and Rezon (vv. 14, 23), and Jeroboam was made Solomon's opponent by a prophet (vv. 29-39).

11:14-22 *Hadad.* The narrative about Hadad is an important source of Edomite history. Either at the time of the initial conquest of Edom by David and Joab (2 Sam. 8:13-14; cf. the superscription to Ps. 60) or following the suppression of a subsequent revolt, Hadad, of the royal house of Edom, escaped and eventually found refuge in Egypt. There he was well received and married the sister of Pharaoh's wife. Hadad's son Genubath, like Moses, was reared at court with the sons of Pharaoh. Trade with Arabia and the east coast of Africa was an important concern to Egypt, and friendship between the pharaoh and an Edomite prince would have been seen as furthering that interest. This unnamed pharaoh may also have felt that a kingdom in Palestine as powerful as Solomon's was a threat to Egypt's interests. Upon the death of David and Joab (and therefore early in Solomon's reign), Hadad secured reluctant leave from his Egyptian host and returned to his native land to rule in defiance of Israel. However, Hadad's rule must have been confined to a limited portion of Edom and his opposition of a guerilla nature, for Solomon was able to carry on his commercial enterprises through Ezion-geber in Edomite territory apparently without interruption.

11:23-25 *Rezon.* Ironically, David's victory over the Aramean kingdom of Zobah, situated between the Lebanon and Anti-Lebanon ranges (2 Sam. 8:3-12; 10), prepared the way for the

rise of Damascus, which became a deadly foe to Israel. Following
David's conquest of Zobah, Rezon—who had served its king,
Hadadezer—gathered a private army, and "they went to Damascus, and dwelt there" and made Rezon king (1 Kgs. 11:24).
Damascus had been brought under control by David, and Israelite
troops had been garrisoned there (2 Sam. 8:6). Since there is no
mention of conquest by Rezon, it appears that his initial assumption of power was peaceful and with Israelite consent. Did Rezon
pretend to be a friend of Israel and a local ruler with no ambitions
of his own? Whatever the initial course of events, Rezon became
"an adversary of Israel all the days of Solomon, doing mischief as
Hadad did; and he abhorred Israel" (1 Kgs. 11:25).

11:26-40 *Jeroboam.* Solomon's third opponent was Jeroboam,
the son of Nebat and Zeruah ("leper," probably a deliberate
corruption, possibly of Zeruiah, to cast aspersion). Nebat apparently died while Jeroboam was a youth, for his mother is further
identified as a widow (v. 26). Jeroboam impressed Solomon by
his "great energy" (NEB; this seems best to capture the meaning
of *gibbor hayil* in this context) and industriousness, and Solomon
placed him in "charge over all the forced labor of the house of
Joseph," that is, Ephraim and Manasseh (v. 28). In particular,
Jeroboam seems to have supervised the building of the Millo (v.
27; cf. 9:15, 24). Some time after his appointment Jeroboam
"lifted up his hand against the king" (11:26, 27). The story of
Jeroboam has been curtailed in favor of Ahijah's prophecy so that
the text in its present form does not tell us the occasion or reason
for Jeroboam's revolt. The context implies that it was because of
Ahijah's prophecy. The upshot of the revolt was that Solomon
sought to kill Jeroboam, who fled and found refuge with Shishak
of Egypt (v. 40), the first pharaoh to be named in the Bible.
Shishak's reign (ca. 935-914 B.C.) establishes an important cross-
reference in biblical history and enables us to place the disaffection
between Solomon and Jeroboam late in Solomon's reign.

While God "raised up" Hadad and Rezon as adversaries of
Solomon, there is no indication that they were aware of their role
in divine providence (cf. Isa. 45:1-4). Jeroboam, who was to play
the most important role as adversary, is made fully conscious of his
part in God's purposes by the prophet Ahijah from Shiloh. Charac-

teristic of a prophet, Ahijah appears abruptly, without introduction or explanation, and seeks out Jeroboam in the open country as he goes out from Jerusalem. In a symbolic act to dramatize and set in motion his prophecy, Ahijah tears a new garment into twelve pieces, bids Jeroboam take ten of these, and interprets the meaning of his actions to be that the LORD is about to rend Solomon's kingdom asunder and to give Jeroboam ten of the tribes (1 Kgs. 11:30-31)— Jeroboam is Solomon's unnamed servant of v. 11! This action is accounted for, in terms that correspond to and elaborate vv. 11-13, as judgment on Solomon for his apostasy (vv. 32-36). Ahijah concludes by promising Jeroboam rule over the ten northern tribes, God's presence, and a sure house if he would be responsive and obedient as David was (vv. 37-38).

THEOLOGICAL REFLECTIONS ON 11:14-40

It would be interesting to know how a secular historian contemporary with the author-editor of 1–2 Kings would have treated the breakup of Solomon's kingdom. He probably would have emphasized the political, economic, and military factors and taken into account the leadership ability of Hadad, Rezon, and Jeroboam. It is doubtful that he would have seen any moral purpose in the rebellion of Hadad, Rezon, and Jeroboam or that God was involved in any way. Fundamental to biblical theology in general is the understanding that the events of our lives and the destiny of nations are an intelligible drama under the sovereign, purposeful direction of God. To be sure, the divine sway in human life and destiny is not always comprehensible. Job is never given an explanation for his malady. Jeremiah experiences profound inner turmoil, doubt, and despair (Jer. 12:1-6; 15:10-21; 17:14-18; 18:18-23; 20:7-13, 14-18), and the author of Ecclesiastes boldly declares that "all is vanity" (Eccl. 1:2; 12:8). But God's questions from the whirlwind (Job 38–41) direct Job's attention to the marvelous design and providence in nature and invite Job to trust that God cares and that life has meaning even though he cannot discern it. The very fact that Jeremiah shares his confessions with us is proof of his triumph over despair, and the author of Ecclesiastes admits that although the meaning of life is inscrutable everything is "in the hand of God" (Eccl. 9:1).

The audience to whom 1–2 Kings is addressed knew well the

ambiguities, enigmas, and contradictions of life. They had witnessed the fall of the northern kingdom, the great reform of King
Josiah, the undoing of that reform, the crushing defeat of Judah by
the Babylonians, and exile. A basic concern of the author-editor of
1–2 Kings is to affirm God's sovereign control and purpose precisely in the midst of the turbulence of history. He sees God's
providence embracing high (Solomon) and low (Jeroboam), Israelite (Solomon and Jeroboam) and foreigner (Hadad and Rezon),
even when the foreigner is an enemy of Israel (cf. Amos 9:7). He
declares, moreover, that God makes his will and purpose known
through his word which he vouchsafes to his prophets (1 Kgs.
11:29-39; cf. Amos 3:7), a word that with irresistible power shapes
history. God's promises do not fail (1 Kgs. 8:56). What is uttered
by God's mouth is fulfilled by God's hand (8:24; cf. Jer. 23:29; Isa.
55:10-11). Indeed, the history of Israel and Judah according to the
author-editor of 1–2 Kings is a record of prophecy and fulfillment
(cf. Gerhard von Rad, *Studies in Deuteronomy,* ch. 7).

For a secular historian the collapse of Solomon's kingdom
would undoubtedly have been regarded as an unfortunate turn of
fate. To the author-editor of 1–2 Kings it was evidence of the
righteous rule of God and a cause for hope and praise (cf. Josh.
7:19; Amos 4:13; 5:8-9; 9:5-6).

The passage is also a reminder of how fragile all human power is
(Isa. 40:15, 23-24). During Solomon's heyday people must have
thought his kingdom would endure a thousand years. The united
kingdom of David and Solomon lasted just two generations!

THE END OF SOLOMON'S REIGN (11:41-43)

The long account of Solomon's reign is concluded with a citation
of the chief literary source used and brief notices about the length
of Solomon's reign (forty years), his death and burial, and the
name of his son and successor (Rehoboam).

The major source used in preparing the account of Solomon's
reign was the Book of the Acts of Solomon, whose contents
consisted of the "acts of Solomon, and all that he did, and his
wisdom" (1 Kgs. 11:41). This work would seem to have been a
factual, "secular" work lauding Solomon and giving detailed

information about the royal palaces, government buildings, construction of the Millo, store-cities, fortifications, tax records, trade and diplomatic agreements, Solomon's wisdom, and so forth. The author-editor of 1 Kings has used the Book of the Acts of Solomon selectively and supplemented it with other unnamed sources. His contribution, primarily theological and from a Deuteronomic point of view, will have been:

(1) the prominence given to the temple;
(2) the establishment of Solomon's succession and building of the temple as the fulfillment of Nathan's prophecy in 2 Sam. 7;
(3) the emphasis on obedience and the centrality of the First and Second Commandments;
(4) the divine gift of wisdom as the basis of Solomon's achievements;
(5) the interpretation of the reason for the dissolution of Solomon's kingdom; and
(6) the structure of the account of Solomon's reign.

THEOLOGICAL REFLECTIONS ON SOLOMON THE MAN

Solomon made a significant contribution to the history and religion of Israel, but he was no saint. He was wise, ambitious, amorous, enterprising, shrewd, peace-loving, luxury-loving, harsh, oppressive, and in the end his heart was not "wholly true" to God. The author-editor of 1 Kings, while fully aware of Solomon's failings, has drawn Solomon's portrait so as to express appreciation for his achievements. This effect is accomplished by selection and emphasis. To prevent the negative side of Solomon's character from overshadowing his positive contribution, the treatment of his sin is deferred to the end of the account of his reign and his old age (ch. 11). The portrait of Solomon is sketched against the background of a panorama of a vast, teeming kingdom of prosperity, strength, and peace. In the foreground sits Solomon, clothed magnificently and surrounded with splendor, his countenance radiating wisdom. The most prominent object, however, is the temple. It is the real center of the canvas and that which gives unity to the composition. Solomon belongs to that vast company of flawed characters with which the Bible and the Church abound and with whom God must work daily to achieve his purposes.

94

PART II
THE ESTABLISHMENT OF THE NORTHERN KINGDOM

1 Kings 12:1–14:20

Following the long and outwardly glorious reign of Solomon, deep divisions and suppressed grievances surfaced, and the kingdom that seemed so secure broke up overnight. The northern tribes revolted and established themselves as a separate kingdom under Jeroboam. God sanctioned the founding of the new kingdom and its beginning was full of promise, but Jeroboam's policies doomed it from the outset.

THE REVOLT OF THE NORTHERN TRIBES
1 Kings 12:1-20

Almost two hundred years after it happened, Isaiah refers to the event narrated in this passage as the greatest tragedy that had yet befallen the Davidic dynasty (Isa. 7:17). It was certainly a political disaster. With the revolt of the northern tribes, a kingdom that had been a major power was abruptly reduced to two minor states. Yet the account of the breakup of the united kingdom is free of hand-wringing and partisanship. It is treated with such objectivity, in fact, that scholars cannot agree whether it is told by one sympathetic to Rehoboam and Judah or to Jeroboam and the northern tribes. The special role of the Davidic dynasty in divine providence and the desirability of a united kingdom are presupposed, but the cause of the northern tribes is presented as just and their breaking away is treated sympathetically. The passage strongly condemns repressive government, but it does not romanticize revolt.

THE ASSEMBLY AT SHECHEM (12:1-5)

The occasion for this fateful moment in Israelite history was an assembly of "all Israel" (i.e., the fully represented northern tribes; 1 Kgs. 12:3, 16, 18, 19, 20) at Shechem to make Rehoboam king. Rehoboam's succession as king in Judah (11:43) took place without incident and calls for no comment. But the house of David ruled over a dual monarchy (Judah and Israel), and Rehoboam's kingship over Israel required a separate ceremony, presumably the renewal of the covenant made between the northern tribes and David (2 Sam. 5:1-3). The elders of Israel came to Hebron to negotiate the original covenant with David, but Rehoboam went to Shechem. The context suggests that Rehoboam went not on his own initiative but at the insistence of the northern tribes.

Located some 66 km. (41 mi.) N of Jerusalem and situated between Mt. Ebal and Mt. Gerizim, Shechem was rich in historic associations. Shechem was the place where God appeared to Abraham and promised him the land of Canaan (Gen. 12:1-7), where Jacob settled after his sojourn with Laban (Gen. 33:18-20; 34), where Joseph was buried (Josh. 24:32), where Joshua made a covenant with Israel (Josh. 24), and where the covenant was periodically renewed (Deut. 11:26-32; 27:1-26; 31:9-13). By insisting that Rehoboam come to this famous site located in their territory, the northern tribes asserted their distinct identity within the covenant people. They were willing to accept Rehoboam as king, but they demanded respect for their cultural and theological traditions and the redress of certain grievances.

The appearance of unity among the twelve tribes during the period of the judges and earlier is deceptive (cf. Judg. 5). While the details of tribal history cannot be fully reconstructed, it is generally agreed that Judah and Israel had related but distinct historical experiences in Palestine. As a result they developed different theological traditions in much the same way as Protestant and Catholic Christians (cf. Murray L. Newman, Jr., *The People of the Covenant*). In Israel the Exodus event, Sinai covenant, conquest tradition, and the democratic institutions of the period of the judges became normative. The foundation stones of Judah's theological traditions were God's covenant with David, his choice of Zion, and the institution of the monarchy. Rehoboam was accepted as king in Judah by right of primogeniture. But the spirit of charismatic leadership from the time of the judges lived on in Israel. There it was felt that the people had a voice in determining who would be king and that they had rights he must respect (1 Sam. 11:12-15; 12; 15; 2 Sam. 3:17-21; 5:1-3).

The demands of the northern tribes are reasonable, even modest: "Lighten the hard service of your father and his heavy yoke upon us, and we will serve you" (12:4). For the first time we learn how Solomon's rule was perceived by the northern tribes. It was oppressive. The sources of grievance in particular would have been the burden of forced labor and taxation disproportionately borne by the northern tribes (see above on 4:7-19).

Having heard of the conditions of the northern tribes, Rehoboam dismissed the assembly for three days to consider them.

REHOBOAM TAKES COUNSEL WITH
HIS ADVISORS (12:6-11)

Rehoboam first consults the advisors who had served Solomon (cf. 4:1-19). They counsel Rehoboam to consent to the demands of the northern tribes in order to secure their continued loyalty. Rehoboam should "be a servant" (i.e., fulfill his role as one who represents and is responsible to God) and "serve" the people (12:7). This advice does not please Rehoboam, however, and he forsakes it even before he hears the counsel of another group of advisors, "the young men [literally, 'boys'] who had grown up with him" (v. 8) and with whom he identifies. "What do you advise that *we* answer this people?" he asks. Their counsel is to reject contemptuously the demands of the northern tribes. They urge Rehoboam to say, "My little finger is thicker than my father's loins. And now, whereas my father laid upon you a heavy yoke, I will add to your yoke. My father chastised you with whips, but I will chastise you with scorpions," that is, spiked lashes that sting and cut the flesh (vv. 10-11).

REHOBOAM'S DECISION AND
THE REVOLT OF ISRAEL (12:12-20)

When the assembly is reconvened, Rehoboam, "forsaking" (repeated for emphasis, cf. v. 8) the counsel of the experienced advisors, speaks harshly and as his "boy" advisors had urged (vv. 12-14). Israel answers with a traditional rallying cry that gives vent to its pent-up distrust:

What portion have we in David?
    We have no inheritance in the son of Jesse.
To your tents, O Israel!
    Look now to your own house, David. (v. 16; cf.
2 Sam. 20:1)

With these words the assembly breaks up in disarray, and Solomon's kingdom is rent asunder, never to be made whole again.

In a clumsy effort to save the situation Rehoboam sends Adoram, the head of forced labor, perhaps to explain more fully the terms of forced labor and possibly to offer some concession.

But he is stoned to death, and Rehoboam has to make a hasty departure (1 Kgs. 12:18). "And when all Israel heard that Jeroboam had returned, they sent and called him to the assembly and made him king over all Israel" (v. 20), thus asserting their democratic tradition of kingship.

The account of the assembly at Shechem is supplemented by three notes. Verse 15 interprets Rehoboam's refusal to hearken to the northern tribes as "a turn of affairs brought about by the LORD that he might fulfill his word, which the LORD spoke by Ahijah the Shilonite to Jeroboam the son of Nebat." Verse 17 points out that after the division of the kingdom a number of Israelites already dwelling in Judah for various reasons accepted Rehoboam's kingship and remained there. Verse 19 is the comment of a Judahite made some time before the fall of Israel in 722 B.C.: "So Israel has been in rebellion against the house of David to this day." Whereas vv. 1-16 portray Israel's bid for independence as provoked by Rehoboam's arrogance and blundering, here it is viewed as treasonable disloyalty against legitimate authority *(pasha')*.

The text does not present a clear picture of the role of Jeroboam. According to vv. 2-3a, 12a he was present from the outset and participated in the negotiations, but according to v. 20 the northern tribes turned to him only after the negotiations had broken down. A possible explanation is that v. 2 originally referred to Jeroboam's response upon hearing of the death of Solomon. The "it" he heard was later understood to be the assembly at Shechem; vv. 2-3a were recast to make this clear, and Jeroboam's name was added in v. 12. If this is correct, v. 20 gives the true picture of Jeroboam's role. On the other hand, the confused account of Jeroboam's activities may simply reflect the turbulence of the proceedings at Shechem.

THEOLOGICAL REFLECTIONS ON 12:1-20

Rehoboam's behavior is a classic example of arrogant power. He and his youthful advisors are indignant at the thought that the governed have rights. They view governmental power as the king's personal prerogative to be imposed at will. The stoning of Adoram and the threatening anger toward Rehoboam reveal how deepseated were Israel's grievances. By ignoring this and rejecting the counsel of his older advisors, Rehoboam emerges as insensitive, arrogant, foolhardy, and politically stupid.

While human folly played its part in the breakup of the kingdom, ultimately "it was a turn of affairs brought about by the LORD" (v. 15). This is not to say that God caused Rehoboam to act as he did. There were many ways Ahijah's prophecy could have been fulfilled. As Joseph's brothers meant their treatment of Joseph for evil but God meant it for good (Gen. 50:20), so Rehoboam's free act is integrated into divine providence.

How great was the promise of Israel in the days of Solomon! As the most powerful kingdom in Palestine-Syria, with the temple built and worship flourishing, the conditions were ideal for Israel to make their witness felt. As Samson squandered his great strength, so Israel squandered their great opportunity. The matter-of-fact manner in which this failing is treated must be because the narrator knows how endemic such failings are among the people of God.

A PROPHET RESTRAINS
REHOBOAM
1 Kings 12:21-24

Arrogant power caused the division of the kingdom. But the offender characteristically feels himself to be the offended, and so Rehoboam determined to heal the breach in the kingdom by enraged, vengeful power. Upon returning to Jerusalem he assembled a large army and was poised to go to war with Israel. Over against him and his army stood a lone man, Shemaiah, "the man of God" (a synonymous term for a prophet, cf. 1 Kgs. 13:18; 2 Kgs. 5:8; 2 Chr. 12:5). Shemaiah's word to Rehoboam and his army was that they should not go to war against "your kinsmen" (literally, "brothers"), for the division of the kingdom was in accordance with God's will. Rehoboam presumably had the military advantage, and had he acted quickly and decisively he might well have suppressed the revolt of Israel. It is to his credit that he heeded the word of Shemaiah. While 1 Kgs. 14:30 speaks of continual warfare between Rehoboam and Jeroboam, this was confined to disputes over their common border rather than all-out war.

THEOLOGICAL REFLECTIONS ON 12:21-24

Since this encounter took place in Jerusalem, Shemaiah was presumably a Judahite. It is necessary to be aware of this to appreciate what he did. Shemaiah's message goes against the perceived national interest, opposes a popular cause, and stifles the impulse to avenge wounded pride. But Shemaiah was a man of God before he was a man of Judah. His loyalty to God transcended that to king and country. His identity came from his relationship to God, not from society. He served God rather than the state. In short, he was a prophet. Because of Shemaiah we have one of those rare moments in history when peace prevailed—if only briefly (14:30)—over war.

Not to be overlooked is the change in Rehoboam's behavior. The brash, arrogant man of 12:1-20 hearkens to Shemaiah and desists from the campaign to restore the kingdom. In his fifth year he saved Jerusalem and Judah from being plundered by Pharaoh Shishak by paying a large ransom (14:25-26). Even a Rehoboam can amend his ways! That a profound change took place in Rehoboam is hinted at by the fact that the people are blamed for the sin of Judah during Rehoboam's reign (14:22-24; but cf. 15:3).

JEROBOAM ESTABLISHES HIS KINGDOM

1 Kings 12:25-32

Of the seven verses of this passage, one is devoted to Jeroboam's building activities and six to his religious innovations—a revealing disclosure of where the interest of the narrator lies. In contrast to the objectivity of 12:1-20, this passage is clearly from a Judahite who assumes that a Davidic king is the true sovereign of all the covenant people, that Jerusalem is the proper place of worship, and that levitical priests are the only legitimate ones.

JEROBOAM'S BUILDING ACTIVITIES (12:25)

Jeroboam first chose Shechem for his capital and "built" (i.e., fortified) it; then "he went out from there and built Penuel" on the Jabbok River (Gen. 32:22-31) in Gileadite territory. Did Jeroboam abandon Shechem for Penuel in order to protect himself from Pharaoh Shishak, who invaded Palestine in the fifth year of Rehoboam's reign (1 Kgs. 14:25-28)? Or did Jeroboam fortify Penuel in order to secure Israelite control over Gilead because of its strategic location on Israel's eastern flank? Later Jeroboam moved his capital to Tirzah (14:17), 10 km. (6 mi.) NE of Shechem and famous for its beauty (Cant. 6:4).

JEROBOAM'S RELIGIOUS REFORMS (12:26-32)

The account of Jeroboam's religious reforms is prefaced by a look into the workings of his heart. Jeroboam reasons that if his people continue to worship at the temple in Jerusalem their hearts will "turn again to their lord, to Rehoboam king of Judah, and they will kill me and return to Rehoboam, king of Judah" (1 Kgs. 12:26-27). What is most significant about this disclosure is what is missing. Jeroboam was granted no divine revelation nor was he entrusted with a commission to undertake his reforms. They sprang from his own heart, and he was motivated solely by political considerations and fear. The counsel he takes in v. 28 is with himself (the Hebrew verb is reflexive): "after giving thought to the matter . . ." (NEB).

Foremost of Jeroboam's innovations was the creation of national shrines at Bethel and Dan and the introduction at each of a new cult object, a golden bull, contemptuously called "calf" (vv. 28-29). To the narrator this was a serious departure that "became a sin" (v. 30; cf. 2 Kgs. 10:29). Not only did Jeroboam shatter the religious unity of the people; he is also charged with introducing idolatry and polytheism. He is alleged to have given homage to the golden "calves" themselves: "Behold your gods, O Israel, who brought you up out of the land of Egypt" (1 Kgs. 12:28; cf. v. 32; Exod. 32:4, 8). It is doubtful, however, that Jeroboam thought of the bulls as idols or that he intended to introduce polytheism. The ways of sin are more subtle. Such a flagrant violation of the First and Second Commandments would have made Jeroboam unacceptable as a leader. Moreover, there is no prophetic denunciation of Jeroboam's cult objects before the time of Hosea (Hos. 10:5; 13:2). They were not condemned by the anonymous man of God from Judah at the time of Jeroboam's initial sacrifice at Bethel (1 Kgs. 12:33–13:10), or by Elijah, Elisha, Micaiah ben Imlah, or Amos. Most significantly, they were not removed in the religious purge of Jehu (2 Kgs. 10:29).

With the division of the kingdom, the chief symbol of God's presence, the ark and the cherubim, was left to Judah. Needing a comparable symbol for his new state, Jeroboam chose the bull, universally admired for its strength and procreative power (Deut. 33:17; Isa. 10:13; 34:7; Ps. 68:30; 1 Kgs. 7:25). It is probable that Jeroboam meant the bull to serve the same function as the ark and cherubim, that is, as the throne or footstool of the invisibly present God.

It is also unlikely that Jeroboam intended to introduce polytheism. The text hints at a dedication of both bull images at Bethel (12:32), followed by a procession in which "the people went before the one to Dan" (v. 30 MT; the RSV follows the Lucianic recension of LXX). If both bull images were dedicated at Bethel, "gods" could have been part of the language of that ceremony. Otherwise, the narrator or a later scribe has intentionally made the reference to the deity plural in v. 28 and treated the bulls as idols in order to place responsibility on Jeroboam for the actual practice of polytheism and idolatry that did develop in his kingdom.

The rest of Jeroboam's innovations are simply listed, although the narrator's disapproval is unmistakable (vv. 31-32). In addition to founding the national shrines at Bethel and Dan, Jeroboam (1) promoted worship at local sanctuaries (high places), (2) created a new priesthood "from among all the people, who were not of the Levites," (3) altered the festal calendar by moving the Feast of Booths from the seventh month as it was celebrated in Judah (Lev. 23:34-36) to the eighth month, (4) officiated as priest at Bethel, and (5) installed priests from the high places there. The aversion to priests who were not Levites and the condemnation of worship not centered at Jerusalem and not in accord with its festal calendar identify the narrator as one whose sympathies are with Judah and the levitical priests.

THEOLOGICAL REFLECTIONS ON 12:25-32

While the narrator is highly critical of Jeroboam, it is not unlikely that Jeroboam thought of himself as a progressive, enlightened leader and that he was so regarded by many in his kingdom. The adoption of the bull as a cult object may have been an effort to adapt the ark and cherubim to the culture of the northern tribes, especially since the bull was an indigenous symbol to the Canaanite element of the population. Archaeological finds in Palestine-Syria of statues depicting a god astride a bull point to a function for the bull similar to that of the ark and cherubim (*ANEP,* nos. 470-501, 522-538). Moreover, Jeroboam espoused the classic confession of Israel's faith: God is the one who brought Israel up out of the land of Egypt; he is the one who identifies with the oppressed and intervenes to liberate them (1 Kgs. 12:28). The two cult sites had ancient, hallowed associations. Bethel was founded by Jacob (Gen. 28:10-22; 35:1-15), and the priesthood of Dan went back to a grandson of Moses (Judg. 18:30).

David had appointed Levites "for all the work of the LORD and for the service of the king" (1 Chr. 26:30-32) and had placed them in strategic locations, especially among the non-Israelite elements of his kingdom (cf. Josh. 21:1-42 and Benjamin Mazar, "The Cities of the Priests and the Levites"). Jeroboam understandably would have felt that levitical priests, owing loyalty as they did to the house of David and noted for their zeal (Gen. 49:5-7; Exod. 32:25-29), would have been subversive of his rule had they been allowed to remain in office.

Agricultural seasons and traditions vary, and it is possible that the changing of the date of Booths was simply the endorsement of popular preference among the northern tribes.

Few people have been as well prepared to rule as Jeroboam, and few have had such a promising beginning. His industry, efficiency, and leadership were such that he quickly rose to a leading position in Solomon's bureaucracy. God singled out Jeroboam to be the ruler of the oppressed northern tribes, and Ahijah designated him as such, making promises to him comparable to those made to David. Inspired by Ahijah, Jeroboam "lifted up his hand against" Solomon in protest against the oppressive treatment of the labor brigades from Israel, and his protest was so forceful that he had to flee for his life to Egypt (1 Kgs. 11:26, 27, 40). His Egyptian experience would have broadened him and further prepared him to govern. After the breakdown of the negotiations with Rehoboam at Shechem, Jeroboam was the inevitable choice of the northern tribes to be their king. Yet this able, attractive man with such promise came to be regarded as a villain who was chiefly responsible for the ruin of Israel. And this ruin is traced directly to his religious innovations.

Whereas the innovations of David and Solomon were undertaken as a result of divine initiative and under divine guidance, those of Jeroboam were the product of fear. They were introduced on his own initiative and were for the purpose of securing his own rule (cf. Amos 7:13). Then, too, Jeroboam was incredibly naive. "Bull" was a favorite epithet for El, head of the Canaanite pantheon, and for Baal. The high places were the stronghold of Canaanite traditions and practices. A clergy not steeped in Israelite values was ill-equipped to keep Israel true to its destiny in the inevitable accommodation between Israelites and the large numbers of Canaanites in Jeroboam's kingdom. Jeroboam's religious innovations were an invitation for the identification of Baal and the LORD and for the assimilation of Canaanite ways and values. Slowly, imperceptibly, Israel's religion became alloyed, lost its true character, and "became a sin."

The story of Jeroboam is the story of a good man gone wrong. It is the story of a man who protested the abuses of power only to be seduced by power, a man whose concern for others gave way to concern primarily for himself, who came to feel that the welfare of his people depended more on their loyalty to him than to God. He who had been called by a prophet to be the instrument of God's purpose used religion as the instrument of his own purpose. What had been entrusted to him as a gift and responsibility he tried to make a possession. In his effort to secure himself, he opened the way for his own and the nation's destruction.

CONDEMNATION OF WORSHIP AT BETHEL

1 Kings 12:33–13:34

This strange story forms the centerpiece of the account of Jeroboam's reign. Although Jeroboam is the major character, center stage is occupied by two anonymous prophets. Wonder and miracle abound. Jeroboam's hand is paralyzed and healed, and a lion stands docilely by its victim but does not consume. The story also shocks and offends, for it presents one prophet deliberately lying to another. The action develops in unexpected ways, and the meaning of it all is veiled until the very end. When the meaning is disclosed, it provides the key for understanding the fate of Jeroboam and his kingdom.

THE PROPHECY AGAINST THE ALTAR AT BETHEL (12:33–13:10)

The passage opens with Jeroboam preparing to celebrate the Feast of Booths by offering sacrifices on the "altar which he had made in Bethel" on the new date, the eighth month, which he "had devised out of his own heart" (1 Kgs. 12:33). The context suggests that this was the dedication of Bethel as a national shrine of Israel. Just as Jeroboam is poised to offer sacrifices, a man of God from Judah abruptly appears to denounce the altar (12:33–13:1).

Politically, Israel and Judah were now separated, but they shared a common religious heritage that permitted the man of God from Judah to cross political boundaries (as Amos also did). He did so because the religious unity and identity of the covenant people were threatened by the new center of worship at Bethel. It was especially at the three annual pilgrimage festivals celebrated by all Israel at a common central sanctuary that Israel's sense of unity, identity, and destiny was nurtured (Exod. 23:14-17; 34:18-24).

The bringing of the ark to Jerusalem and the building of the temple were premised on the understanding that Jerusalem was now the divinely chosen central sanctuary for all Israel. From the point of view of a Judahite then, the bull image at Bethel, the non-levitical priesthood, and the celebration of the most important annual festival at another site than Jerusalem and at another than the traditional time posed a serious threat to the spiritual integrity of the covenant people. But the man of God from Judah went not on his own initiative; he was "moved by the word of the LORD" (1 Kgs. 13:1 NEB).

Addressing the altar directly and speaking for the LORD, the God of all the covenant people, the man of God declares that the altar is doomed to desecration by a descendant of David named Josiah who will sacrifice and burn the bones of the priests of the high places upon it (v. 2).

In situations of unusual significance and urgency a present, tangible pledge, a sign *(mophet),* is sometimes added to a prophecy to confirm its genuineness and the certainty of its fulfillment. To impress on Jeroboam the futility of his religious innovations and to assure him that the prophecy against the altar at Bethel would come to pass, the man of God announces a sign: "Behold, the altar shall be torn down, and the ashes that are upon it shall be poured out" (13:3).

The identification of Josiah as the agent of desecration and the specification of precisely how he would carry it out are generally thought to have been added in light of the measures Josiah took against Bethel almost three centuries later (2 Kgs. 23:15-20). Prophets normally address themselves to the present and immediate future and rarely name names or prophesy in such specific detail.

The prophecy and the sign so alarm Jeroboam that he orders the man of God arrested on the spot. But the hand of human authority stretched out in anger withers and becomes impotent (1 Kgs. 13:4). Royal authority is no match for prophetic authority. It is next reported that the sign confirming the prophecy takes place. The altar is torn down, and its ashes, saturated with the fat devoted to God, are spilled on the ground, rendering the fat unclean (Lev. 6:8-11) and the sacrifice invalid, a portent of the vanity of worship at this altar (1 Kgs. 13:5). The sign moves

Jeroboam to accept the authority of the man of God and to request: "Entreat now the favor of the LORD your God, and pray for me, that my hand may be restored to me." His appeal is honored, and miraculously his hand is restored (v. 6).

Jeroboam then invites the man of God to have a meal with him and offers to reward him. But the man of God refuses, explaining that he has been commanded not to eat or drink while on his mission or to return by the way he came. Obedient to this command, he sets out for Judah by another route (vv. 7-10). The text does not discuss Jeroboam's motive for his invitation. In light of his subsequent behavior (v. 33), most likely he intended to capture the man of God with kindness and favor and so to annul his prophecy.

THE OLD PROPHET OF BETHEL TESTS THE MAN OF GOD FROM JUDAH (13:11-32)

The scene shifts abruptly to the home of an old prophet in Bethel, and the story takes a surprising turn. The sons of the old prophet have just returned from the encounter between the man of God from Judah and Jeroboam and report to their father all that transpired. After ascertaining the route the Judahite man of God had taken, the old prophet follows after him, finds him sitting under an oak, and after establishing his identity invites him to return and eat with him. The man of God from Judah declines and explains, as he had to Jeroboam, the divine constraint he was under about dining. Incredibly, the old prophet of Bethel overcomes the Judahite's objections by identifying himself also as a prophet and by declaring that "an angel spoke to me by the word of the LORD, saying, 'Bring him back with you into your house that he may eat bread and drink water'" (v. 18)! Without further protest or inquiry, the Judahite accepts.

During the meal at the old prophet's home, the Bethelite receives a word from the LORD concerning his guest and communicates it to him: "Thus says the LORD, 'Because you have disobeyed the word of the LORD, and have not kept the commandment which the LORD your God commanded you, . . . your body shall not come to the tomb of your fathers'" (vv. 21-22). Following the meal, the Bethelite saddles the ass of his Judahite guest (for the first and only time called a prophet), who sets out for home and on the way is killed by a lion. The lion, however, does not eat him or attack the ass, but with the ass remains standing beside the body, sentinels of an event both mysterious and awesome. This striking tableau attracts the attention of travelers, and the news of it is brought to Bethel (vv. 23-25). Then the story takes another unexpected turn.

When the old prophet of Bethel hears of the unidentified corpse companioned by an ass and a lion, he knows immediately who it is and what has happened. "It is the man of God, who disobeyed the word of the LORD; therefore the LORD has given him to the lion, which has torn him and slain him, according to the word which the LORD spoke to him" (v. 26). Without delay he goes to the slain man, brings him back to Bethel, mourns him, and buries him—a remarkable burst of energy for one who apparently felt indisposed to attend the dedication of Jeroboam's altar. Then he gives instructions to his sons that when he dies he is to be buried with his colleague from Judah, "For the saying which he cried by the word of the LORD against the altar in Bethel, and against all the houses of the high places which are in the cities of Samaria, shall surely come to pass" (v. 32). In the light of this statement the behavior of the Bethelite prophet becomes intelligible, and the veil of obscurity before this strange sequence of events is finally lifted.

The news of the condemnation of the national shrine of the new state of Israel by the man of God from Judah would naturally have been of concern to every Israelite citizen and especially to their spiritual leaders. There was the possibility that the Judahite prophet was part of a political conspiracy to overthrow the infant sister state. The Bethelite prophet may also have been stirred by feelings of professional jealousy at the intrusion of an outsider into his sphere of influence. In any case, because he was a prophet he had to take seriously a prophecy proclaimed so courageously and reinforced by a sign. It was vital to him to find out whether or not the prophecy of the man of God from Judah was genuine.

If the Judahite could be induced to disobey the prohibition against eating and drinking and there were no consequences, this would prove that he was without divine mandate and that his prophecy had no power. Thus it was precisely the death of the man of God that proved that he acted under divine authority and that his prophecy would be fulfilled. This is why the news of the unidentified corpse on the way to Judah made such an impact on the old prophet of Bethel. And it is because he knew that the man of God from Judah was a true prophet that he brought him back to his house, mourned him, and buried him in the family tomb. The Bethelite's saddling of the Judahite's ass before sending him on his way is a poignant touch, indicating that the old prophet anticipated the fate of his colleague (cf. v. 13).

THE REASON FOR THE FATE OF JEROBOAM AND HIS KINGDOM (13:33-34)

These verses form an epilogue to the preceding narrative and assess Jeroboam's subsequent behavior in the light of it. Jeroboam had personally been witness to a prophecy against worship at Bethel, and the validity of this prophecy had been established in his presence. As if this were not enough, the prophecy had been further confirmed by the death of its bearer, accepted, and affirmed by a native prophet of Jeroboam's kingdom. Moreover, the tomb of the man of God from Judah and the old prophet of Bethel served as a constant reminder of God's disapproval of the altar at Bethel. What plainer and more compelling statement of the divine intent could have been given? In spite of this, Jeroboam incredibly "did not turn from his evil way" but persisted in his determination to maintain a rival center of worship to Jerusalem. He also persisted in the equally harmful practice of promoting worship at the high places led by a priesthood indiscriminately chosen. "Any who would, he consecrated to be priests of the high places" (v. 33; cf. 12:31).

The prophecy against the altar at Bethel is dealt with in such detail and given such a prominent place because Jeroboam's persistence in his ways in spite of it proved to be his undoing. "And this thing became sin to the house of Jeroboam, so as to cut it off and destroy it from the face of the earth" (v. 34).

THEOLOGICAL REFLECTIONS ON 12:33–13:34

This passage raises many complex and difficult issues, among them tolerance of competing forms of belief and worship, obedience, and lying. Israel and the Church have vacillated between permissive indifference and arrogant suppression of all that does not conform to their norms in faith and practice. Both extremes are to be avoided, but the experience of the kingdom of Israel is a case in point that choices about these matters do make a difference. The northern tribes are no more. (The Israelites of today are descendants of Judah and those who identify with them, i.e., Jews.) The basic reason for the fall of the northern kingdom according to 1–2 Kings is that king and people were too open and accepting of alien values and practices (2 Kgs. 17:7-23). The one responsible for this fateful development was Jeroboam, who opened the way for it with his religious innovations.

There is no more ringing affirmation in the Bible of the importance of obedience, particularly in "little things," than in the tragic fate of the man of God from Judah. He was heroic in obedience to the command to deliver—at great risk to himself—the prophecy against the altar at Bethel, but accepted too readily the alleged revelation of another that contradicted the revelation God had given him. The authentic word of God often seems extreme and unreasonable, and how adept we are in finding reasons to disobey it. The fate of the man of God from Judah is also a word of the LORD, namely, that obedience is a matter of life and death. The focus on "little things" emphasizes by contrast the importance of obedience in "big things."

The lie of the old prophet of Bethel, especially since he receives a revelation from God after it, raises some hard questions. There is a subtlety in the claim of the Bethelite that would have aroused the suspicion of an alert person. He attributes the authority for his invitation not directly to God but to an angel (1 Kgs. 13:18). This does not excuse the lie, and the passage is no brief for lying (cf. Exod. 20:7, 16; 23:7; Lev. 19:11; Ps. 119:163; Prov. 12:22; Jer. 7:9; Hos. 4:2; Zech. 8:16-17; Matt. 5:33-37; Col. 3:9; Rev. 21:8). Rather, the Bethelite's lie should be seen as a lack of resourcefulness and moral maturity by one intent on determining the true character of the prophecy against the altar at Bethel.

The passage is a powerful exposé of the seriousness of persisting in a wrong course of behavior when one knows better. Jeroboam's religious reforms were wrong, but there was still hope for him. The prophecy against his altar and its confirmation by the two prophets was an urgent summons to him to "turn from his evil way," but he refused. The problem of Jeroboam was not that he was ignorant of God's will, but that he knew it and ignored it. That was also the problem of the rich man in the parable of Lazarus (Luke 16:19-31)—and of humankind through the ages. The tomb of the man of God from Judah and the old prophet of Bethel stands as a brooding, accusing witness against Jeroboam—and human willfulness.

Finally, the passage is an eloquent testimony to the power of God's word. Jeroboam tries to suppress, subvert, and ignore it; the Judahite man of God who delivers it is disobedient; and the old prophet of Bethel verifies it with a lie. But in spite of everything, it triumphs. Even death confirms it, and a tomb becomes its memorial.

JEROBOAM AND AHIJAH: THE SECOND ENCOUNTER

1 Kings 14:1-18

The career of Jeroboam is framed by encounters with the prophet Ahijah of Shiloh that profoundly shape his destiny. The first (1 Kgs. 11:29-39) sets Jeroboam on the road to the kingship of Israel; the second, narrated in the present passage, settles the fate of his dynasty and kingdom. Much has happened since the first encounter. Jeroboam's capital is now at Tirzah (14:17). Ahijah has become old and blind, impaired in body but not in mental and spiritual faculties. In the meantime, Jeroboam has become alienated from Ahijah so that he dares not approach him in person. But there comes a time when Ahijah is the only person to whom Jeroboam can turn.

THE PILGRIMAGE OF JEROBOAM'S WIFE TO AHIJAH (14:1-6)

The occasion that compels Jeroboam to seek Ahijah is the illness of his son, Abijah. It appears that Abijah, presumably the heir apparent, was a person of unusual promise, for when he died all Israel mourned him (v. 18). The name Abijah means "Yah(weh) is my father," additional evidence that Jeroboam did not think of himself as abandoning the worship of the covenant God, Yahweh/the LORD (see above on 12:28-30).

The estrangement between king and prophet is so deep that not even illness can overcome it. So Jeroboam instructs his wife to disguise herself as an ordinary citizen and take a gift of ten loaves of bread, some cakes, and a jar of honey and go to Ahijah and consult him about their son (cf. 1 Sam. 9:7-8; 2 Kgs. 5:15; 8:8). Despite the alienation, Jeroboam does not doubt Ahijah's power: "He will tell you what shall happen to the child" (1 Kgs.

14:3). What he hopes for, of course, is a word from the prophet that would effect the healing of his son. And he does not hesitate to try to manipulate that outcome.

In obedience to Jeroboam's instructions, his wife, disguised and with gifts in hand, makes her way to Ahijah's house in Shiloh. God shows his disapproval of this attempt to take advantage of his prophet by disclosing all to him. Before the queen can consult Ahijah concerning her son, the prophet announces that he is "charged with heavy tidings" for her (v. 6).

AHIJAH'S FIRST ORACLE (14:7-11)

Ahijah's message to Jeroboam is formulated in two speeches (vv. 7-11 and vv. 12-16). The first is a prophecy of the overthrow and eradication of Jeroboam's dynasty. Speaking as the LORD's messenger, Ahijah first gives the reasons why the dynasty will be cut off (vv. 7-9). In a word, Jeroboam has not kept God's commandments, particularly the First and Second. He has not followed God with his whole heart as David did, and he has made other gods and molten images (the golden calves). This is all the more offensive in that God had elevated him to kingship at the expense of the Davidic dynasty.

The announcement of judgment (vv. 10-11) that follows from these reasons is pictured in slashing language and imagery that emphasize the completeness of the extermination of Jeroboam's dynasty. "Every male" is a euphemistic paraphrase of the Hebrew (cf. KJV). "Whether still under the protection of the family or not" (NEB) is preferable to "both bond and free" (RSV), since the focus is the royal family. The house of Jeroboam will be as utterly consumed as one "burns up dung until it is all gone" (v. 10). Worst of all, the family will be denied burial and their corpses left for dogs and carrion birds to scavenge on (v. 11), a profoundly disturbing prospect for a person of the ancient world (cf. 1 Sam. 31:10-13; 2 Sam. 21:8-14; 2 Kgs. 9:34-37; Virgil *Aeneid* vi.282-383).

AHIJAH'S SECOND ORACLE (14:12-16)

The second speech is given on Ahijah's own authority and has three parts. First, Ahijah announces the death of Abijah, who ironically is the only worthy member of Jeroboam's family (1 Kgs. 14:12-13). Second, Ahijah states that the LORD will raise up the founder of a new dynasty in Israel who will cut off the house of Jeroboam (v. 14). Finally, Ahijah prophesies the defeat and exile of the northern kingdom. Israel, he says, will be smitten with instability "as a reed is shaken in the water," uprooted from the good land God gave their fathers, and scattered beyond the Euphrates (v. 15). Why? Because the people made Asherim (images of the Canaanite mother goddess) and because of Jeroboam's sins. Although Jeroboam "made Israel to sin," his example and authority do not annul individual responsibility.

THE RETURN OF JEROBOAM'S WIFE AND THE DEATH OF ABIJAH (14:17-18)

As Jeroboam's wife comes to the threshold of her house in Tirzah, her son dies as Ahijah had prophesied. Abijah's death is also a portent of the fulfillment of the rest of the "heavy tidings" she bears. All Israel mourns Abijah, a tribute to him personally, and perhaps an indication that his father still enjoys considerable popular support. Ahijah does not represent a consensus of opposition to Jeroboam; he speaks for God.

THEOLOGICAL REFLECTIONS ON 14:1-18

Because of his experience with oppressed workers under Solomon, Jeroboam's rule may have been enlightened, progressive, and humane. If we had a complete record of his administration it might well contain impressive social reforms. But according to this passage the basic source of good government is wholehearted commitment to God and obedience to his will. Without these, however innovative and promising the policies and programs, government becomes the mask of human will and ambition. The passage destroys all illusions about naive, good intentions. Jeroboam may not have intended to introduce idolatry and polytheism, but he might as well have, for they are directly related to his reforms. Tragically, the one who could have been the father of his country comparable to David (11:38) cast God behind his back (14:9), "made Israel to sin" (v. 16), and thus condemned his dynasty and kingdom.

119

The judgment on Jeroboam and on Israel is a reminder that the aggrieved and the reformer are also subject to sin and are responsible to the same authority to which they appeal in their protest. Those who act in the cause of justice and righteousness are not exempt from the subtle temptation to identify their own will with the divine will and to try to manipulate God and God's prophet to serve their self-interest. But to appeal to the prophet who elevates to office is to come under the authority of one who removes from office. God is against the oppressor, but he is not bound to the reformer.

Ahijah's announcements of judgment are one of the most powerful statements of the seriousness and awful consequences of sin in the Bible. Sin provokes God to anger (vv. 9, 15), and when the people persist in sinning despite solemn warnings (ch. 13) it leads to overthrow and exile. Indeed, the basic affirmation of the passage is that sin is the most powerful negative force shaping human life and destiny. If we had access to the Book of the Chronicles of the Kings of Israel (14:19) and other contemporary sources, modern historians would most likely debate the sociological, political, and economic reasons for the overthrow of Jeroboam's dynasty and the fall of the northern kingdom. For the biblical writer there was no mystery about these events. Whatever contributing factors there may have been, the root cause was sin. Moreover, sin is not a private, individual matter whose consequences are confined to the sinner; it is communal and generational. Jeroboam's sin dooms both his dynasty and his kingdom, his innocent son and unborn generations.

There is an obverse side to the harsh judgment on Jeroboam. As parents discipline a wayward child because they love the child, so God's anger and judgment are the expression of a passionate caring. The greatest cruelty of all would be for God to ignore us in our sin. The very starkness with which the awful consequences of Jeroboam's sin are presented is meant as a warning, an urgent call to repentance, a summons to keep God's commandments and to follow God with all one's heart as David did (v. 8).

CONCLUDING SUMMARY AND OBITUARY

1 Kings 14:19-20

All the political events of Jeroboam's reign are summarized in the phrase, "how he warred and how he reigned." For additional information the reader is referred to "the Book of the Chronicles of the Kings of Israel," the second named source to be utilized in 1 Kings (cf. 11:41; 14:29). The stories about Ahijah and the man of God from Judah and the old prophet of Bethel would have come from prophetic circles. Despite his sin and in contrast to his descendants (vv. 11, 13), Jeroboam is granted the dignity of being buried in the family tomb. The narrator leaves us to draw our own conclusions about this grace.

PART III

FROM THE DEATH OF SOLOMON TO THE BEGINNING OF THE REIGN OF AHAB

1 Kings 14:21–16:28

The first half century of the separate Israelite states was dominated by rivalry and civil war. This period is of interest to the author of 1 Kings primarily as forming the background to the reign of Ahab and the prophets who were active at that time, chief among whom was Elijah. The period is surveyed dutifully but sparsely, with sixty-two verses devoted to the reigns of eight kings.

FORM AND STYLE

The narrator introduces a new format and style at this point that enables him to state the essence of a king's reign with an economy of words. The introduction and conclusion of the account of each reign conform to a fixed pattern with only slight variations. The following information is regularly given in the introduction to the reigns of the kings of Judah: (1) date of beginning of reign, (2) age at beginning of reign (not noted consistently at first), (3) length and place of reign, (4) name of the queen mother, and (5) a theological evaluation. The pattern for the Israelite kings is the same except that their ages and the names of their mothers are not given. The reign of each king, both Judahite and Israelite, is normally concluded in this manner: (1) summary of reign and referral to the royal annals for additional information, (2) notice of death and place of burial, and (3) name of successor.

The body of the account of a king's reign has no fixed form, but is built up from materials selected from the royal annals, temple archives, and prophetic narratives. The amount and kind of material naturally varies from king to king. More than half of these sixty-two verses consists of introductions and conclusions.

Set phrases and formulas abound in 14:21–16:28. As literature this portion of 1 Kings is not elegant. At best there is a certain liturgical flow in the patterned sequence of reigns. It is an efficient way to outline and summarize.

DATING AND CHRONOLOGY

Not having a fixed calendar to work with, the author-editor dates the beginning of the reign of each king in relation to the contemporary monarch of the sister kingdom. The Judahite kings are taken up first and dated in relation to Jeroboam of Israel. Then the narrator shifts to the Israelite kings and relates them to the forty-one-year reign of Asa of Judah. On the basis of the chronology worked out by Edwin R. Thiele *(The Mysterious Numbers of the Hebrew Kings)* and adopted in this study, the accession dates of the Judahite and Israelite kings from the death of Solomon to the beginning of the reign of Ahab are:

Judahite kings		Israelite kings	
Rehoboam		JEROBOAM	931 B.C.
Abijam ———>		18th year,	913
ASA ———>		20th year,	911
2nd year	←———	Nadab	910
3rd year	←———	Baasha	909
26th year	←———	Elah	886
27th year	←———	Zimri	885 (7 days)
31st year	←———	Omri	881

DEVELOPMENTS IN JUDAH (14:21–15:24)

Three Davidic kings reigned during this period: Rehoboam (931-913), Abijam (913-911), and Asa (911-870). All three were engaged in civil war with Israel throughout their reigns. The chief source of contention was the border between the two states, particularly between Jerusalem and Bethel, which are only 16 km. (10 mi.) apart. Each kingdom sought to gain an advantage for itself, and the border see-sawed back and forth throughout most of this period before it was finally stabilized. For the most part these were minor skirmishes, and they are referred to in general summary statements. "There was war between Rehoboam and Jeroboam continually" (14:30, repeated at 15:6), between Abijam and Jeroboam (v. 7), and between Asa and Baasha "all their days" (v. 16, repeated at v. 32).

Hostilities between Judah and Israel were halted temporarily by an external threat to both. In the fifth year of Rehoboam (the first dated international event in the Bible) Pharaoh Shishak conducted a compaign against Palestine, apparently aimed primarily at taking booty. Rehoboam paid a huge sum, including Solomon's golden shields (14:25-27), and Jerusalem and Judah were spared. Jeroboam evidently resisted, for among the more than 150 cities Shishak claims to have plundered many are located in Israel, including Transjordan (*ANET,* 242-43, 263-64). It may be conjectured that Rehoboam's fortification of fifteen cities (2 Chr. 11:5-12) and Jeroboam's building of Penuel (1 Kgs. 12:25) are related to Shishak's invasion, either in anticipation or as a result of it.

When Shishak withdrew he apparently stationed or reinforced a garrison of Ethiopian troops (2 Chr. 12:2-3) at Gerar in southwestern Palestine, for it was from Gerar that a large Ethiopian army led by Zerah invaded Judah during the reign of Asa (2 Chr. 14:9-15; cf. William F. Albright, "Egypt and the Early History of the Negeb"). Ethiopians were still at Gerar during the reign of Asa's grandson when the LORD stirred up against Jehoram (848-841) "the anger of the Philistines and of the Arabs who are *near* the Ethiopians" (2 Chr. 21:16). The Ethiopians of Africa were not near the Philistines and Arabs, but those at Gerar were. Finally, during the reign of Hezekiah (715-686) the Simeonites added Gerar (reading "Gerar" with LXX for MT "Gedor"; cf. JB, TEV) to their territory, displacing the Ethiopians and Meunim, an Arabian people (1 Chr. 4:39-41; cf. 2 Chr. 20:1-23; 26:7). By the time of Hezekiah, Ethiopians would have been at Gerar for at least two centuries. Presumably Egypt lost control of Gerar following the reign of Shishak, and the Ethiopian troops stationed there settled down and became farmers, for the Simeonites "found rich, good pasture, and the land was very broad, quiet, and peaceful; for the former inhabitants there belonged to Ham" (1 Chr. 4:40).

According to 1 Chr. 4:41, the Simeonites exterminated the Ethiopians and Meunim of Gerar, but this is traditional language and not to be taken literally (compare Josh. 10:40-42; 11:11, 14, 20, 21-23 with Judg. 3:1-6; Ezra 2:43, 50; Neh. 7:46, 52). Are the Black Arabs of the Jordan Valley descended from the Ethiopians and Meunim of Gerar (cf. M. S. Seale, "The Black Arabs of the Jordan Valley"; and John W. Wenham, "The Black Arabs of the Jordan Valley")? The surviving Ethiopians and Meunim of Gerar would have been incorporated into the population of the Simeonites and would have become a part of the racial and ethnic amalgam of other Ethiopians or Cushites (Num. 12:1; 2 Sam. 18:19-33; superscription to Ps. 7; Jer. 36:14; 38:7-13; 39:15-18; Zeph. 1:1), Egyptians (Gen. 41:45, 51-52; 48:3, 5; 1 Kgs. 3:1),

Canaanites (Gen. 38; Judg. 3:1-6), Arameans (Deut. 26:5), Amorites and Hittites (Ezek. 16:3), Philistines (2 Sam. 15:18-22), Moabites, Ammonites, Edomites, and Sidonians (Ruth; 1 Kgs. 11:1; 16:31) who made up the people of Israel.

During the reign of Asa (911-870), Israel gained a decisive advantage over Judah when Baasha (909-886) fortified Ramah, only 9 km. (5.6 mi.) N of Jerusalem, thereby gaining control of access to Jerusalem from the north and the west (1 Kgs. 15:17). (Zerah's invasion of Judah from the south during Asa's reign may be related to Baasha's seizure of Ramah, possibly at Baasha's instigation.) With funds from the treasuries of the temple and palace, Asa induced Ben-hadad, king of Syria, to form a league with him "as between my father and your father" and to break his alliance with Baasha (vv. 18-19). Ben-hadad "hearkened to King Asa," invaded the upper Jordan Valley, and conquered "Ijon, Dan, Abel-beth-maacah, and all Chinneroth, with all the land of Naphtali" (v. 20). Syria's policy evidently was to play off one Israelite state against the other so as to keep both weak.

Syria's intervention enabled Asa to push the border a few kilometers eastward to Geba and northward to Mizpah and thus to place Jerusalem in a more secure position (v. 22). But the advantage gained was bought at a dear price. Syria had grown strong since the time of Rezon (11:23-25; possibly identical with Hezion, the grandfather of Ben-hadad, 15:18), and Ben-hadad's conquests whetted an appetite that was to make Syria a deadly rival to both Israel and Judah.

The legacy of Solomon was not only political disruption but also religious apostasy. During the reign of Rehoboam the people of Judah built high places and set up pillars and Asherim. Both male and female cult prostitutes were involved in worship. (*Qadesh* in 14:24 should probably be understood collectively, contrary to the RSV, for cult prostitutes were of both sexes; cf. Deut. 23:18.) In general there was a lapse into "all the abominations of the nations which the LORD drove out before the people of Israel" (1 Kgs. 14:23-24).

These practices persisted during the reign of Abijam, taxing the patience of God. Were it not for the merit of David, Abijam might not have been spared. "Nevertheless for David's sake the LORD his God gave him a lamp in Jerusalem, setting up his son after him, and establishing Jerusalem" (15:4). Judah was rescued from this downward spiral by Asa, who carried out a thorough reform. He put away the cult prostitutes, removed the idols, and displaced Maacah from her influential position as queen mother "because she had an abominable [pornographic?] image made for Asherah" (vv. 11-15).

DEVELOPMENTS IN ISRAEL (15:25–16:28)

Six Israelite kings were contemporaries of Rehoboam, Abijam, and Asa: Jeroboam (931-910), Nadab (910-909), Baasha (909-886), Elah (886-885), Zimri (885, 7 days), and Omri (885-874). The disparity between these numbers is due to a series of revolts in Israel. Baasha assassinated Jeroboam's son Nadab and exterminated Jeroboam's house, thus fulfilling the prophecy of Ahijah (15:27-30). But Baasha also "did what was evil in the sight of the LORD, and walked in the way of Jeroboam" (v. 34), and Jehu the son of Hanani announced the overthrow of his dynasty (16:1-4, 7). When Baasha's "playboy" son Elah remained at the capital carousing while his troops were in the field at Gibbethon, Zimri, a chariot commander, struck him down. Zimri had no prophetic backing or popular support, however, and within seven days Omri, commanding general of the army, overthrew him (vv. 9-20). Rivalries between branches of the military or between "modernists" and "conservatives" or possibly because of Omri's background (there is no mention of his family or tribe) prevented Omri from being acceptable to all. "Then the people of Israel were divided into two parts; half of the people followed Tibni the son of Ginath, to make him king, and half followed Omri" (v. 21). This state of affairs continued for some four years (vv. 15, 23), in the course of which "the people who followed Omri overcame the people who followed Tibni the son of Ginath; so Tibni died [violently? or naturally?], and Omri became king" (v. 22).

From the standpoint of secular history, Omri was one of the ablest of the kings of Israel. He reunified a people divided by a long civil war and established the first dynasty in the northern kingdom to endure beyond the first generation. In a move comparable to David's choice of Jerusalem, Omri purchased Samaria as his private holding and there created a new capital for Israel (v. 24). Centrally located, easy to defend, and without previous tribal ties, Samaria rapidly became the pride of the northern kingdom and the symbol of its identity (Isa. 28:1-4).

The most critical problem facing Israel at this time was to control the growing power of Syria. Omri dealt with this brilliantly. He ended the war with Judah so that he might concentrate his military forces against Syria. This may be inferred from the lack of any reference to war with Judah during Omri's reign and from the fact that Ahab, Omri's son, and Jehoshaphat of Judah were allies (1 Kgs. 22). Next, Omri formed an alliance with Phoenicia, sealing it by the marriage of Ahab and Jezebel, daughter of Ethbaal, king of the Sidonians (16:31). Finally, Omri "afflicted Moab many days" (Moabite Stone, 4-5; *ANET,* 320-21), occupying the northern part of that country and exacting an annual tribute of "a hundred thousand lambs, and the wool of a hundred thousand rams" (2 Kgs. 3:4).

Omri's greatness in the eyes of the world is attested by the respect shown to him by the Assyrians, the most powerful state in the biblical world at this time. In their inscriptions, Israel is referred to as "the land of Omri" and Jehu, who founded another dynasty, is called "son of Omri" (*ANET,* 280, 281, 284, 285). All Omri is credited with in 1–2 Kings is the founding of Samaria, and only six verses are devoted to his reign (1 Kgs. 16:23-28).

In religion and morality there was a downward spiral in Israel as well as Judah, but instead of being corrected by reform, it went unchecked, gaining momentum from dynasty to dynasty. The fundamental sin of the northern kingdom was the sin of Jeroboam, that is, the disruption of the unity of the covenant people and accommodation to Canaanite ways and values. All the kings of Israel "walked in the way of Jeroboam and in his sin which he made Israel to sin." Characteristic of sin, it got worse as it spread. Baasha and Elah added their own contribution to Jeroboam's sin (16:2, 7, 30), and Omri and Ahab did "more evil than all who were before" them (vv. 25, 30). It was this alarming escalation that required the intervention of Elijah and other prophets.

POLITICAL DIFFERENCES BETWEEN JUDAH AND ISRAEL

Comparing the political histories of the two kingdoms, one is struck by the turmoil in Israel and the stability in Judah. There were three violent disruptions of government and a civil war in Israel. In Judah, by contrast, the succession was orderly and routine.

The reasons for the differences are geographical, political, and theological. Judah was relatively isolated, cut off from the coastal plain by the Philistines and from Transjordan by the Dead Sea. Israel, on the other hand, was neighbor to Syria and Phoenicia, and the major thoroughfares of Palestine passed through its territory, linking Israel to the larger biblical world and making it vulnerable to political developments there. Ethnically and culturally Judah was comparatively homogeneous. Israel with its ten tribes and large Canaanite population (Judg. 3:1-5) had a history of tribal rivalries (Judg. 8:1-3; 12:1-6) and had to contend with differing culture patterns. There were also basic differences in the understanding of kingship.

God's covenant with David and his dynasty (2 Sam. 7; 23:1-7; Ps. 89:3-4, 17-37; 1 Kgs. 15:4-5) insured political stability in Judah. Davidic kings also had the advantage of reigning in Jerusalem, "the city which the LORD had chosen out of all the tribes of Israel, to put his name there" (14:21; cf. 8:16, 44; 11:13; 15:4). Among the northern tribes, however, there was deep-seated distrust of royal power (Deut. 17:14-20; Judg. 8:22-23; 9:7-15; 1 Sam. 8:4-22; 12), and there the traditions of the nonhereditary, limited power of the charismatic leaders of the tribal confederacy lived on. In keeping with these traditions, prophets played an active role in politics, having the authority to raise up and to overthrow kings. The volatile political climate of the northern kingdom also lent itself to exploitation by the ambitious and unscrupulous, as by Zimri.

The greatest danger to the covenant people during this time came not from an external enemy nor from political instability, but from Canaanite religion. What made it so attractive and why was it such a threat?

CANAANITE RELIGION

There are numerous references to Canaanite religion in the OT, but they are scattered and fragmentary. Fortunately, the biblical material is supplemented by a number of Canaanite religious texts dating from about 1400 B.C. (*ANET,* 129-155), discovered in

1929 at Ras Shamra (ancient Ugarit) in northern Syria. The chief concern of Canaanite religion was fertility. Its mythology celebrates how Baal, "Rider of the Clouds" and god of rain and storm, became the chief source of fertility and supreme among the gods. Baal was thought to be indispensable to vitality in nature. When the earth languished for want of rain it was because Baal was slain by Mot, the god of sterility and death. When life was restored to nature it was because Baal was rescued and revived by his sister Anath, the goddess of love and war. Fertility was understood as a divine force released by sexual union between Baal and his consort, variously identified in the OT as Asherah (plural, Asheroth; Judg. 3:7; 6:25; 2 Kgs. 23:4) or Ashtoreth (plural, Ashtaroth; Judg. 2:13; 10:6; 1 Sam 7:3-4; 12:10). The divine couple could be activated from the human realm by sexual relations with a cult prostitute.

In the larger cities the chief Canaanite gods were worshipped in temples but in the smaller cities and villages at high places. A high place would be typically located on a hill apart from the city and in a grove of trees (e.g., Deut. 12:2; 1 Sam. 9:25; 10:5; 1 Kgs. 14:23; 2 Kgs. 17:10; Jer. 2:20; Hos. 4:13). Upon a raised platform there would be an altar and nearby an Asherah tree or pole, a stone pillar apparently representing Baal (2 Kgs. 3:2; 10:26, 27), a banquet hall, and possibly other buildings (1 Sam. 9:22; 1 Kgs. 13:32). At the high places the worshippers would assemble, drink wine (Hos. 4:11; Amos 2:8), eat raisin cakes (Hos. 3:1), and engage in sex with cult prostitutes (Hos. 4:13-14; Amos 2:7-8; Jer. 3:6, 23) in the name of securing increase in field, flock, and family.

THEOLOGICAL REFLECTIONS ON 14:21–16:28

By paring down this segment of history to the bare bones, the author of 1 Kings gives the most revealing insight thus far into his historiography. He is well informed about those matters that interest modern historians, such as building activities (1 Kgs. 15:22-23; 16:24), diplomatic alliances (15:17-19), conspiracies (vv. 27-29; 16:9-20), invasions (14:25-26; 15:20), wars (14:30; 15:6, 7, 16, 32; 16:21-22), and even the ailments of a king (15:23), but all these are only of incidental interest to him. The author is an interpreter of history who sees the two most powerful forces shaping human life and destiny as sin and the word of God. The chief sin is violation of the First and Second Commandments, which provokes God to jealousy (14:22) and anger (15:30; 16:2, 7, 13, 26). The consequences are political violence and overthrow. But sin can be mastered (Gen. 4:7) by repentance and reform (1 Kgs. 15:9-15). Through his prophets God gives his word to shape and interpret the course of events by identifying sin and announcing the penalty for it (vv. 29-30; 16:1-4, 7, 12-13).

1 Kings is not the work of an ivory tower theoretician; it deals with real facts and is addressed to those who had experienced political shipwreck. The historiography of Kings instructs us to look to the spiritual and moral roots of political unrest, decline, or disaster, and it provides a remedy for political health.

Political leaders are responsible in a special way for their moral conduct and for the spiritual well-being of God's people (16:2). That which from a secular point of view is regarded as impressive and important about a ruler is largely ignored, noticeably so in the case of Omri. The first responsibility of a leader is spiritual and moral intregrity, and the true criterion of his or her leadership is a people whose lives are ordered by God's commandments. Each king, Judahite and Israelite, is evaluated theologically. The ideal is for the king's heart to be "wholly true" to God, as Asa's was, and for him to do what is right in the eyes of the LORD (15:14). The model in this respect was David, and he is the standard by which others are measured (3:3, 6; 9:4; 11:4, 6, 33, 38; 14:8; 15:3, 5, 11; 2 Kgs. 14:3; 16:2; 18:3; 22:2). It was also the king's responsibility to correct harmful developments, even if it meant going against the queen mother. And it was the duty of Judahite kings to maintain the purity of Jerusalem (Ps. 101).

The difference between the fate of Israel and Judah, in fact, was determined by their kings. At the beginning of this period Judah experienced under Rehoboam and Abijam an outbreak of paganism that made it little different from Israel. But before Judah reached the point of no return it was rescued by the reforms of Asa. The kings of Israel, however, persisted in the way of Jeroboam, driving Israel deeper and deeper into sin, and all are condemned. Both kingdoms were confronted with a decision between life and death. Because of Asa, Judah chose life.

Canaanite religion was crass in many ways, but had a poetic, mystical appreciation of nature. On one occasion Baal speaks these words in a message to Anath:

I've a word I fain would tell thee,
     A speech I would utter to thee:
Speech of tree and whisper of stone,
     Converse of heaven with earth,
     E'en of the deeps with the stars;
Yea, a thunderbolt unknown to heaven,
     A word not known to men,
     Nor sensed by the masses on earth. (*ANET,* 136)

The focus on such a vital concern as fertility and the provision for humans to participate in and influence its dynamics gave Canaanite religion an appeal Israelites found difficult to resist. This practical appeal would have been reinforced by the mystical rapport with nature and the eroticism of Canaanite worship.

The temptations of Canaanite religion, in different, more subtle forms, are no less real today than in the past. It is a fundamental urge of human nature to want one's way of life to be supported and enhanced by the divine realm. "Canaanite" religion subverts this need by making one feel that one can manipulate the divine to serve one's self-interest and to support the status quo. Such religion encourages self-centeredness and self-indulgence rather than obedience and service (Hos. 2:12). Emotion is integral to religion, but "Canaanite" religion short-circuits innocent, genuine caring into eroticism and erases the distinction between the two. Celebration is basic to worship, but "Canaanite" religion debases the impulse to rejoice into mindless revelry and debauchery (Hos. 4:11).

PART IV

THE REIGN OF AHAB AND THE PROPHETIC OPPOSITION

1 Kings 16:29–22:40

The stylized, summary treatment of 1 Kgs. 14:21–16:28 now gives way to expansive, vivid narratives that unfold one of the most crucial and dramatic moments in the history of the northern kingdom. Thus far assimilation of Canaanite ways and values had gone on silently and subtly. With Ahab and Jezebel it becomes boldly open, and official recognition is given to Canaanite gods. This crisis calls forth a band of prophets, most notably Elijah and Elisha, who wage a life-or-death struggle for the heart and soul of Israel.

INTRODUCTION
1 Kings 16:29-34

During Ahab's reign Israel experienced unprecedented political stability, strength, and prosperity. Ahab succeeded his father without opposition and renewed the alliances with Phoenicia and Judah. Trade with Phoenicia and tribute from Moab brought great wealth to the nation. Ahab had one of the largest military establishments in Palestine-Syria, fielding 2,000 chariots and 10,000 troops against the Assyrians at the battle of Qarqar in 853 B.C. (*ANET,* 279). Archaeologists confirm a building boom at Samaria, Megiddo, and Hazor during the reigns of Omri and Ahab unsurpassed for excellence of craftsmanship and luxury.

The author of 1-2 Kings ignores these achievements, for according to his theological criteria Ahab did "evil in the sight of the LORD more than all that were before him" (16:30) and did more "to provoke the LORD, the God of Israel, to anger" than all his predecessors (v. 33b). Specifically, Ahab married Jezebel, the daughter of Ethbaal, king of the Sidonians (an inclusive term for the Phoenicians), served and worshipped Baal, built a temple and altar for Baal in Samaria, and made an Asherah (vv. 31-33a; cf. Deut. 16:21). This represents a quantum leap in the history of apostasy.

Appended to the introduction to Ahab's reign is a report of the rebuilding of Jericho (1 Kgs. 16:34). After the conquest of Jericho, Joshua pronounced a curse on anyone who might rebuild it (Josh. 6:26). In arrogant disregard, Ahab had Jericho rebuilt, most likely to strengthen his hold on Moab. The project was supervised by a certain Hiel of Bethel. Both the laying of the foundation of the city and the completion of its gate were marked by the loss of one of Hiel's sons.

Placed at the beginning of Ahab's reign—such information is

138

normally given in the conclusion (1 Kgs. 15:23; 22:39)—this building report portends that Ahab, as the one responsible for the rebuilding of Jericho, also stands under Joshua's curse.

With the king embracing Canaanite religion and the queen aggressively promoting it (ch. 18), what chance did the authentic faith of Israel have of surviving? In a wonderful, mysterious way, however, the LORD had prepared an Elijah to "come to the kingdom for such a time as this" (Esth. 4:14).

ELIJAH AND THE DROUGHT
1 Kings 17:1–19:18

Chapters 17, 18, and 19 center around a great drought that lasted some three years. This material falls into three "acts": the drought as a challenge to Canaanized religion (ch. 17); the confrontation between Elijah and the leaders of Canaanite religion and the ending of the drought (ch. 18); and Elijah in flight and self-examination following his victory (19:1-18). Each "act" has a roughly parallel structure (cf. Robert L. Cohn, "The Literary Logic of 1 Kings 17–19"):

A. An announcement that precipitates a conflict
by Elijah (17:1)   by God (18:1)   by Jezebel (19:2)

B. A journey in two stages
to Cherith (17:2-3)   to Obadiah (18:7)   to Beer-sheba (19:3)
to Zarephath (17:8-9)   to Ahab (18:17)   to Horeb (19:8)

C. Two successive encounters in which feeding is involved
ravens (17:6-7)   Obadiah (18:7-16)   angel (19:5-6)
widow (17:8-16)   Ahab (18:17-20)   angel (19:7)

D. A crisis that is resolved by the intervention of God in power
resuscitation (17:17-23)   fire (18:21-38)   theophany (19:9-18)

E. A conversion and confession of faith in the LORD or renewal
widow (17:24)   Israel (18:39)   Elijah (19:19-21)

ACT I: THE DROUGHT (17:1-24)

ELIJAH'S ANNOUNCEMENT OF THE DROUGHT (17:1)
Like a meteor out of the blue, Elijah bursts upon Ahab's world

140

defying the royal establishment and challenging the powerful mystique of Canaanite religion. All that is told about Elijah's antecedents is that he was from Tishbe in Gilead, traditionally (but not certainly) located at Listib, about 13 km. (8 mi.) N of the Jabbok River.

At the time of his initial encounter with Ahab, Elijah is already a prophet, one who "stands before" (i.e., serves) God. His name, which means "My God is Yahweh," states succinctly the theme of his ministry. In an age characterized by easy tolerance and open assimilation to Canaanite religion, Elijah asserts his personal determination ("My God" is emphatic) to keep the First Commandment. It is to bring the northern kingdom to a like determination that his ministry is directed.

The time, place, and circumstances of Elijah's explosive intrusion into history are not recorded. Everything gives way to the word he proclaims to Ahab, most likely in Samaria: "As the LORD the God of Israel lives, before whom I stand, there shall be neither dew nor rain these years, except at my word." By his reference to "the LORD, the God of Israel," Elijah reminds Ahab that the LORD is the proper God of the covenant people. Elijah also characterizes the LORD in sharp contrast to Baal. The LORD is the living God, not a dying and rising vegetation deity as Baal, and the LORD achieves his purposes, not through sex as in Canaanite religion, but by his word. There could be no bolder challenge to Ahab and his policy of support for Canaanite religion.

Central to Canaanite mythology was the dogma that Baal was the giver of rain. By proclaiming that for an indefinite period ("these years") there would be neither dew (the only source of moisture during the summer) nor rain (which falls from October to March) except by his word, Elijah asserts that Canaanite theology is a lie, that Baal is no god at all. There is nothing tentative about Elijah. He allows for no contingencies, exceptions, or escape clauses, for his challenge, introduced by "as the LORD lives," is in the form of an oath. Elijah's challenge is directed at the heart of Canaanite religion, and he is determined to be victorious.

The rest of the chapter forms an interlude between Elijah's initial challenge and the dramatic contest on Mt. Carmel (ch. 18), in which the progressive worsening of the drought is pictured and suspense builds. This period of time is divided into three episodes arranged in ascending, climactic order: Elijah at the brook Cherith, Elijah and the widow of Zarephath, and Elijah and the widow's dead son.

ELIJAH AT THE BROOK CHERITH (17:2-7)

Ahab's response to Elijah's challenge must have been hostile, for God commands Elijah to "depart from here" (Samaria?) and to hide himself by the brook Cherith east of the Jordan, territory familiar to the prophet and far from the king (17:2-3). This was not the time to risk arrest and execution; Elijah must be free to interpret the meaning of the drought and bring it to an end.

Elijah's stay at Cherith is pictured in a series of silent tableaus rather than in dialogue and action. The scenes are of great austerity and solitude. There is only the diminishing stream, the daily provisioning of the ravens, and Elijah. Or, rather, there is the stream, the ravens, Elijah—and God. The closer one looks at these stark scenes, the clearer there emerges a man of remarkable faith, one who is obedient, who prays for his daily bread, who has learned to live with God as his sole source of help and supply.

There is no indication of how long Elijah remained at Cherith. Because of the long duration of the drought, it must have been several months. It was not merely a time of hiding and waiting; it was also a time of prayer and spiritual preparation. Before Elijah can minister to the widow of Zarephath and face the prophets of Baal on Carmel he must first tarry at Cherith. Before Elijah can inspire faith in others and do his mighty deeds he must first learn to be faithful and to be dependent on the Source of all power. If there were moments of confident trust and sweet communion, there must also have been times of spiritual drought and doubt, but these are known only to God and Elijah.

ELIJAH AND THE WIDOW OF ZAREPHATH (17:8-16)

Although Cherith dries up, this does not exhaust the resources of God and the prophet to cope with the drought. In an unexpected initiative, God directs Elijah to go on a second journey to Zarephath, about 10 km. (7 mi.) S of Sidon, and informs him that there he will be fed by a widow. Zarephath was in Jezebel's home country

(16:31), where Baal was thought to be supreme, and a widow was the weakest, most vulnerable member of society in the biblical world! However paradoxical God's directive may have seemed, Elijah obeys.

As Elijah arrives at the city gate of Zarephath, he finds a widow gathering sticks (17:10). Elijah must determine by a test of faith if she is the one God had commanded to feed him (v. 9). "And he called to her and said, 'Please get me a little water in a jar, that I may drink.' And as she was going to get it, he called to her and said, 'Please bring me a piece of bread in your hand'" (vv. 10b-11 NASB; RSV alone of modern versions ignores Elijah's politeness). There was still water at Zarephath because it was on the Mediterranean coast, but food was another matter. With a rush of anguished words, spoken with the solemnity of an oath ("as the LORD your God lives"), the widow informs Elijah that she has only enough food left for one final meal (v. 12). Elijah charges the woman to conquer her anxiety ("fear not"), directs her to prepare what she has for him first, and promises her in the name of the LORD, "The jar of meal shall not be spent, and the cruse of oil shall not fail, until the day that the LORD sends rain upon the earth" (vv. 13-14).

Although she was a Canaanite, the woman takes Elijah at his word, prepares the meal as directed, and she and her household are miraculously supplied for many days "according to the word of the LORD which he spoke by Elijah" (vv. 15-16). Here in Baal's backyard, in the home of the weakest member of society, a demonstration of the power of the word of God is given. In contrast to the manipulative sexual rites of Canaanite religion, the word of God, when accepted in faith, is able to supply one's needs even under the most adverse conditions.

ELIJAH AND THE WIDOW'S SON (17:17-24)

Those who live by faith and miracle are not exempt from trouble. The satisfying note on which the preceding episode ends is shattered when the widow's son becomes ill, and "his illness was so severe that there was no breath left in him" (v. 17). The loss was intensified by the fact that the son represented the widow's future security and the continuation of the family name. Grief-stricken and seized with resentment and fear, the mother confronts Elijah. The miracle of the unfailing jar of meal and cruse of oil was obvious proof that he was in touch with the spiritual realm, but for her Elijah's powers had taken on a sinister character. "What made you interfere, you man of God?" (NEB) she asks. Her only explanation for what had happened is that Elijah had sought her out "to bring [her] sin to remembrance, and to cause the death" of her son (v. 18).

Elijah does not defend himself but carries the child to his room on the roof of the woman's house. He, too, has questions, and he puts them to God: "O LORD my God, hast thou brought calamity even upon the widow with whom I sojourn, by slaying her son?" (vv. 19-20; cf. Deut. 32:39; 1 Sam. 2:6; Isa. 45:7). Although Elijah has questions he does not hesitate to act on behalf of the lad. He stretches himself upon the boy three times (cf. 2 Kgs. 4:34-35; Acts 20:10) and prays for the restoration of his life (1 Kgs. 17:21). The bodily contact is apparently to infuse the vitality of the prophet into the lifeless corpse, but the critical element is prayer. The boy revives because "the LORD hearkened to the voice of Elijah" (v. 22).

Elijah then presents the mother with her son, and she confesses, "Now I know that you are a man of God, and that the word of the LORD in your mouth is truth" (vv. 23-24; cf. 2 Kgs. 4:8-37; Matt. 9:18-26; Luke 7:11-17; Acts 9:36-43; 20:7-12).

THEOLOGICAL REFLECTIONS ON 17:1-24

One of the most effective strategies of evil is to seduce people into thinking that good and evil are compatible, that the ways of evil are smart, fashionable, and progressive. This strategy was used very effectively against Israel during the reigns of Omri and Ahab so that it became widely accepted that Canaanite and Israelite religion complemented each other. The true significance of Elijah is that he resisted this insidious development with all his being, insisting that the two religions were incompatible and irreconcilable. Elijah's protest prevented Israelite religion from becoming a homogenized blend of Canaanite and Israelite elements and saved Israel from losing their identity and destiny as God's covenant people. His ministry is a reminder that there are values and practices which biblical religion must reject, and he remains a prime example of the importance of prophetic protest.

Elijah's protest was effective because he was well prepared. Whatever Elijah's previous experience as a prophet, he was given an "intensive course" at Cherith. There Elijah was schooled in obedience, waiting on God for his needs (1 Kgs. 17:5-6; cf. Isa. 40:31; Matt. 6:11, 25-33), and prayer (1 Kgs. 17:20, 21; 18:36, 37, 42). Elijah relied on the word of God in the confidence that it would not return empty (Isa. 55:10-11). With the word of God alone he confronted the power structure of the Israelite state (1 Kgs. 17:1, 16, 24). Elijah was not only a spokesperson of the word; he was himself a living word, proclaiming through his name and life-style his wholehearted and exclusive devotion to God. And he so cultivated God's presence that he brought it near to others (v. 18) and was capable of being an instrument of divine power (v. 22). The best proof of the effectiveness of Elijah's preparation is that he was verified as an authentic man of God and the bearer of God's word by a daughter of the very people he opposed (v. 24).

The central issue raised by Elijah's challenge in v. 1 is: Who is the source of life-giving rain, the LORD or Baal? Initial evidence of the LORD's sovereignty is provided when rain and dew cease at Elijah's word and nature is gripped in sterility and lifelessness (vv. 2-16). The death of the widow's son broadens the issue to include human life as well (vv. 17-24). When the LORD restores life to the widow's son and when Elijah's word ends the drought (ch. 18), the issue is decisively settled in favor of the LORD. The thirst for life continues to be humankind's deepest yearning, and many are the modern equivalents of the Canaanite answer. The tested and proven answer remains the word of God (e.g., Deut. 30:15-20), which in its fullest expression became flesh, defeated death itself, and offers eternal life to all who believe (John 1:1-14; 5:24; 17:2-3; 1 Cor. 15:20-26; 1 John 5:11-12).

While there is a persistent aversion to Canaanites and their religion in 1-2 Kings, it is noteworthy with what sympathy the widow of Zarephath is treated. She graciously fetches a drink of water to Elijah although he is a foreigner and she is on the brink of despair (cf. Matt. 10:42; Heb. 13:2). By insisting that she first prepare food for him, Elijah puts her to a test of faith not many would pass. She takes to heart Elijah's "fear not" and acts upon his "thus says the LORD" that the jar of meal and cruse of oil would not fail "until the day that the LORD [not Baal!] sends rain upon the earth." Like the poor widow who gave two copper coins (Mark 12:41-44), she gives all, and her vulnerability becomes God's opportunity. She is sensitive to the power of evil, fearing that her son's death was caused by some secret sin she had committed. And she has the spiritual perceptiveness and maturity to recognize and acknowledge Elijah as the bearer of the authentic word of God (cf. Deut. 18:15-22). In short, this Canaanite woman is a model of openness to the genuine prophet of God. She shames those who out of partisanship or prejudice reject God's servants because of their origin (Luke 4:24-26).

ACT II: THE CONTEST ON MT. CARMEL (18:1-46)

This is one of the most dramatic chapters in the Bible. The atmosphere is charged by the hardship of a long drought, the ruthless persecution of the LORD's prophets, and the relentless hunt for Elijah. Against this background, Elijah boldly confronts Ahab and engages in a life-or-death contest with 450 prophets of Baal. The chapter is made memorable by vivid scenes: Elijah's sudden appearance to Obadiah, Elijah confronting Ahab, a vast throng assembled on Mt. Carmel, Baal prophets dancing about their altar with blood streaming from them, fire from heaven, a violent storm, and a wild race from Mt. Carmel to Jezreel. On this occasion Israel was awakened from the delusion that they could serve both the LORD and Baal.

GOD'S COMMISSION TO ELIJAH (18:1-2a)

Waiting is very much a part of the life of a prophet, for the prophet does not act on his or her own initiative. According to the context, Elijah would have spent the "many days" (1 Kgs. 18:1) with the widow of Zarephath (17:8-24). The drought is now in its third year. This is an imprecise expression in biblical usage, designating either three full years or one full year and parts of the preceding and following year. The time for waiting is ended when the word of the LORD comes to Elijah giving him his "marching orders."

God's commission to Elijah is quite general. The prophet is to show himself to Ahab and to do so with the knowledge that God will send rain. God does not tell Elijah what to say to Ahab but leaves the implementation of the commission to the prophet. "So Elijah went" emphasizes Elijah's obedience. The time of preparation and hiding is over; the time has come to "go to the king" (Esth. 4:16).

THE EFFECT OF THE DROUGHT ON AHAB (18:2b-6)

The famine is "severe" even in the capital city, Samaria, but Ahab has learned nothing from it. What concerns him most is the preservation of the horses and mules of his large chariot force. As a result, Ahab himself and Obadiah, the officer in charge of the royal palace (cf. 1 Kgs. 4:6), take personal charge of the effort to secure hay. Dividing the land between them, Ahab and Obadiah comb the countryside, searching out "all springs of water" and "all the valleys" (v. 5). The king traditionally claimed the right to the first mowings (Amos 7:1), but in this emergency Ahab and Obadiah wield royal authority to exact from local farmers what precious feed remained, justifying it no doubt on the grounds that national security superseded individual needs. What a contrast to Elijah's concern for the widow and her son!

A parenthetical note explains that although Obadiah served Ahab, he "revered the LORD greatly" and had hidden and fed one hundred prophets of the LORD during their persecution by Jezebel (1 Kgs. 18:3b-4). Thus incidentally an alarming development is disclosed. Evidently the prophets of the LORD (inspired by the example of Elijah?) had resisted Jezebel's promotion of the worship of Baal and Asherah, and Jezebel in turn had violently suppressed them.

THE MEETING OF ELIJAH AND OBADIAH (18:7-16)

Ahab and Obadiah go in opposite directions, so that Obadiah is alone "on the way" when Elijah suddenly presents himself. From Obadiah's opening question (v. 7) and the fact that he has to inform Elijah about hiding the prophets of the LORD (vv. 12b-13), it appears that he does not know Elijah personally. If this is correct, it would have been the dress (cf. 2 Kgs. 1:8) and the bearing of Elijah that identified the prophet and caused Obadiah spontaneously to fall on his face before him (1 Kgs. 18:7). Elijah crisply confirms Obadiah's recognition and forthwith directs him, "Go, tell your lord, 'Behold, Elijah is here'" (v. 8).

In his emotional and effusive reply, Obadiah reveals for the first time how Elijah was regarded by Ahab. Three times Obadiah exclaims that if he were to deliver Elijah's message without having the prophet in hand Ahab would kill him (vv. 9, 12, 14). Elijah is the most wanted man in the kingdom, and Ahab has been seeking him with a vengeance, not only in Israel but in neighboring states as well (vv. 9-10). A report of Elijah's words without the prophet himself—and nowhere to be found because the spirit of the LORD would have whisked him to some unknown place—would be criminal negligence in the eyes of the exasperated Ahab. Appealing to Elijah's sympathy, Obadiah informs him how he gave shelter and food to one hundred of the LORD's prophets (v. 13). Elijah subdues Obadiah's fears with an oath taken in the name of "the LORD of hosts," a term out of Israel's past (1 Sam. 1:3, 11; 4:4; 17:45) and expressive of the amplitude of God's sovereign power (NIV renders, "Lord Almighty"), to show himself to Ahab "today" (v. 15). With this assurance Obadiah goes to Ahab, and the meeting of the prophet and the king is set.

THE CONFRONTATION BETWEEN ELIJAH AND AHAB (18:17-19)

The scene shifts abruptly to an undisclosed locale. All circumstantial details are omitted, and attention is centered on the dialogue between king and prophet. It is charged with feeling and tension. Ahab: "Is it you, you troubler of Israel?" Elijah: "I have not troubled Israel; but you have, and your father's house, because you have forsaken the commandments of the LORD and followed the Baals" (vv. 17-18).

The identity of the troubler is always one of the first issues to be raised in a dispute. Ahab apparently assumes that Elijah has offended Baal and that Baal in his wrath has brought about the drought. Elijah is therefore responsible for all the hardship caused by the drought. With a courage difficult to imagine, Elijah denies the king's charge and turns it back on him. The LORD has caused the drought because Omri and Ahab were leading Israel to spiritual disaster.

Elijah boldly follows up his countercharge with the demand that Ahab call an official assembly made up of representatives of all the tribes to meet on Mt. Carmel (v. 19a; cf. 12:1-20). Elijah asks Ahab also to summon to the assembly the 450 prophets of Baal and the 400 prophets of Asherah "who eat at Jezebel's table" (18:19b). To eat at the table of the king or queen was to be subsidized by the state (cf. 2 Sam. 9:9-11; 1 Kgs. 2:7). So aggressive is Jezebel that she promotes at state expense the worship of Baal and Asherah. The passage also reveals incidentally that Phoenicia had prophets as well as Israel (cf. 2 Kgs. 10:19). The unspoken assumption is that the purpose of the assembly is to settle the dispute between Ahab and Elijah.

ELIJAH'S CHALLENGE TO ISRAEL AND THE PROPHETS OF BAAL (18:20-24)

When the action begins again a vast throng has gathered on Mt. Carmel, a long ridge that abuts and forms a "thumb" on the coastline just south of modern Haifa. The site of this convocation is traditionally located at el-Muhraqah ("the place of burning"). Once the participants have assembled, Ahab fades into the background, and the spotlight focuses on Elijah as he faces his Phoenician counterparts—one against 450! (The prophets of Asherah play no active part in the events that follow.) Elijah has been waiting for this moment for a long time, and he is well prepared. In the dialogue and action that follow he is the epitome of confidence. Elijah gives every advantage to the Baal prophets and in his disdain for them deliberately handicaps himself. Each step of the proceeding is carefully noted, and we are invited to marvel at Elijah in his finest hour.

To the assembled throng Elijah puts the question, "How long will you go limping with two different opinions?" (1 Kgs. 18:21a). The prophet appears to be using a proverbial saying whose precise meaning eludes translators. Interpreters are divided as to whether *se'ippim* refers to something forked, as the branch of a tree (Moffatt, JB, Fohrer, Gray, DeVries), or is identical with *se'ippim,* "thoughts, opinions" (KJV, RSV, NASB, NIV). (The initial letter of the two words is different in Hebrew.) The second half of the verse establishes the general sense. The people want to have it both ways, to worship both the LORD and Baal. They walk with one foot for the LORD and one foot for Baal, with consequent splayed gait because of the fundamentally different directions of the two religions. Satire gives way to seriousness as Elijah follows up his question with a ringing call to an either-or choice and commitment: "If the LORD is God, follow him; but if Baal, then follow him" (v. 21b; cf. Gen. 35:2; Exod. 32:25-26; Josh. 24:14-15; Matt. 6:24; Rev. 3:15).

That the issue must be stated so sharply indicates how deeply Canaanite religion had penetrated Israelite life and how eroded in practice the First and Second Commandments had become. That the people answered not "a word" confirms the absence of any sense of conflict of loyalties. So oblivious are they to the issue that something drastic must be done.

Elijah, the bold initiator of action throughout the proceedings, proposes to the assembly a contest to determine whether it is the LORD or Baal who is God. Let each party prepare a sacrifice but lay no fire and call on the name of their deity. "The God who answers by fire, he is God" (vv. 22-24a). The representatives of the tribes approve, answering, "It is well spoken" (v. 24b).

THE APPEAL OF THE BAAL PROPHETS (18:25-29)

Supremely confident, Elijah gives the Baal prophets the first turn and allows them their choice of bull so there could be no question of their animal being unacceptable (v. 25). In accompaniment to a limping dance around the altar they had made, the Baal prophets call on Baal from morning until noon, but "there was no voice, and no one answered" (v. 26). At this point Elijah does something shocking for an ancient man: he ridicules Baal. The prevalent attitude was that, although one might not worship the god of another people, its status as a god was taken for granted. Elijah refuses to grant that Baal is a god at all. With devastating satire he likens Baal to one with all the limitations of a mortal being (v. 27). Just as a human cannot hear a call when absorbed in thought, or

busy (NEB, JB, NIV; RSV "gone aside" is taken by some as a
euphemism for going to the toilet; so TEV), or away on a journey,
or asleep, so is Baal. "Elijah's satire in a nut-shell is the raciest
comment ever made on Pagan mythology" (James A. Montgomery, *The Books of Kings,* 302).

Elijah's taunting incites the Baal prophets to a second attempt
to rouse Baal. In frenzied effort they cut themselves "after their
custom with sword and lances, until the blood gushed out upon
them" (cf. Hos. 7:14), and "raved on" (1 Kgs. 18:28-29). Ecstatic
behavior was the distinctive feature of Canaanite prophecy (cf. the
story of Wen-Amon, *ANET,* 25-29). While also a feature of
Israelite prophecy (1 Sam. 10:9-13; 19:18-24), it was the proclamation of the will of God that distinguished the prophets of
Israel. The cutting (forbidden in Israel, Lev. 19:28; Deut. 14:1)
was apparently to compel the attention of Baal. This went on until
the time of the offering of "the oblation," the main daily sacrifice,
about three o'clock in the afternoon (Josephus *Ant.* xiv.4.3; Acts
3:1). The futility of the efforts of the Baal prophets is reported in
refrain-like fashion: "But there was no voice; no one answered,
no one heeded" (1 Kgs. 18:26, 29).

ELIJAH'S APPEAL AND VICTORY (18:30-40)

When Elijah's turn comes—the Baal prophets having taken most
of the day—he gathers the people about him and repairs the altar
of the LORD "that had been thrown down" (v. 30). This is an
intriguing historical fragment in the story of relations between
Israelite and Canaanite religion, implying that Mt. Carmel was
contested ground between the LORD and Baal.

As the westernmost headland in Palestine, Mt. Carmel is the first
and most frequently watered portion of the land and consequently
famous for its fertility. The name itself means "the garden land."
Hence it was an ideal site for a rain-god like Baal and may have been
a center of Canaanite religion long before the Israelite occupation.
While there is no record of it, Carmel presumably came under
Israelite control during the reign of David. Had the altar of the
LORD been "thrown down" by a party in support of Jezebel (cf.
19:10) with the intention of reclaiming Mt. Carmel for Baal?
Whatever the historical circumstances, Elijah's choice of Mt. Carmel

as the site of the contest is extremely bold. So great is his confidence that he gives the Baal prophets the "home court" advantage.

Mt. Carmel was also famous for its caves—some two thousand are to be found here—and possibly it was here that the prophets of the LORD were hiding (18:4, 13). If so, Elijah's choice of Carmel would also have been to rally them.

In contrast to the frantic behavior of the Baal prophets, Elijah proceeds calmly and intentionally. Appealing to the assembly's sense of identity as the covenant people of the LORD, he builds an altar with twelve stones representative of the twelve tribes of Jacob-Israel and dedicates it to the LORD (vv. 31, 32a; cf. Exod. 24:4; Josh. 4). Next, Elijah prepares a trench about the altar, defining the sacred area. The dimensions of the trench are "as great as would contain two measures of seed" (1 Kgs. 18:32b). Possibly the reference is to the depth and breadth of the trench, but the exact meaning of this expression is obscure. Nor is the significance of pouring four jars of water three times on the offering and wood obvious (vv. 33-35). (The water would have come from a spring that is near el-Muhraqah.) Ritual pouring of water is a widely practiced rite to induce rain. The immediate purpose seems to be to heighten the difficulty of the test.

With the sacrifice drenched and the trench filled with water, Elijah's preparations are completed and the dramatic tension reaches its climax. The narrator foreshadows the outcome by mentioning that it is now the time of the offering of the oblation and by calling Elijah for the first time "the prophet" (v. 36a). A proper sacrifice is about to be made by one who properly bears the title of prophet. The resolution of the contest comes through prayer. Addressing the LORD as "God of Abraham, Isaac, and Israel," Elijah petitions, "Let it be known this day that thou art God in Israel, and that I am thy servant, and that I have done all these things at thy word. Answer me, O LORD, answer me, that this people may know that thou, O LORD, art God, and that thou hast turned their hearts back" (vv. 36b-37).

Elijah's prayer defines succinctly the issues at stake between him and Ahab and the purpose of the convocation on Mt. Carmel. Ahab holds that Baal is a true god and that Israel should worship him as well as the LORD. Elijah prays that the LORD alone be proven to be divine and the only deity for Israel. Ahab charged

Elijah with being the troubler of Israel. Elijah asks to be vindicated as the LORD's servant whose conduct in relation to the drought was in obedience to God's word. Ahab and the people are oblivious of anything wrong in worshipping Baal along with the LORD. Elijah knows that they cannot return to the LORD without the LORD's help and prays that they may be made aware of God's grace in turning their hearts back.

Typically, the LORD's response exceeds all expectations. Not only is there a manifestation of fire (cf. Lev. 9:24; 10:2; Num. 16:35; Judg. 13:20), but it "consumed the burnt offering, and the wood, and the stones, and the dust, and licked up the water that was in the trench" (1 Kgs. 18:38). This awesome display of power moves the people to fall on their faces and confess, "The LORD, he is God; the LORD, he is God" (v. 39). Elijah's prayer is answered. The LORD is proven to be divine and is acknowledged as such by the people. Now the way is cleared for the ending of the drought without there being any question as to who is responsible for it. And Elijah is vindicated.

Elijah had prayed that it might be made known that the LORD was God in Israel (v. 36b). Had the Baal prophets acknowledged the LORD's victory, would not Elijah and the assembly have embraced them? But they would not and consequently are slaughtered at Elijah's command (v. 40). Was this done in obedience to one of the laws mandating the death penalty for those who serve or cause others to serve other gods (Exod. 22:20; Deut. 13:1-5, 6-11, 12-18; 17:2-7; cf. Exod. 32:25-29; 2 Kgs. 10:18-28)? In any case, the dispatch of the prophets of Baal would not have been regarded as murder, but as a sacramental purging of evil (cf. Deut. 7:1-5; 13; Josh. 7; 1 Sam. 15; 1 Kgs. 20:42). This way of dealing with offenders falls short of the highest in OT religion (e.g., 2 Kgs. 6:20-23; Isa. 45:18-25) and is resoundingly condemned in the NT (most notably in Matt. 5:43-48; Luke 6:27-36). The episode is a sobering reminder that a noble spiritual victory may be used in ignoble ways, that religious partisans in general do not have a very good record in their treatment of rivals.

THE END OF THE DROUGHT (18:41-46)

While the contest with the prophets of Baal is the most dramatic part of ch. 18, the real climax is the coming of the rain and the ending of the drought (17:1). Ahab's response to the contest is not recorded, but he is the one to whom Elijah primarily directs attention for the ending of the drought. Magnanimous to his former opponent, Elijah invites a silent and subdued Ahab to go up (from where to where is not clear), eat, and drink (18:41a). By this invitation Elijah declares that the time of deprivation is over, that the drought is ended. There is as yet no sign of rain, not even a cloud, but Elijah is so certain of it that he already hears with the ear of faith "a sound of the rushing of rain" (v. 41b). The king accepts without comment the prophet's invitation (v. 42a).

As Ahab eats and drinks, Elijah engages in an intense prayer vigil. As it was through prayer that Elijah achieved his victory over the Baal prophets, so it is through prayer that the drought is ended (cf. 17:1). The prayer that moved God to answer by fire was made publicly and consisted of petitions (18:36b-37). Here Elijah withdraws to a solitary place, squats, and puts his face between his knees. No words are spoken, no petition made, for Elijah already has the assurance that rain is coming (18:1). In incandescent concentration and anticipation, Elijah bids his servant look toward the sea. Seven times the servant goes back and forth between the prophet and a prominent point overlooking the Mediterranean (v. 43). The seventh time he sees "a little cloud like a man's hand . . . rising out of the sea" (v. 44). Immediately Elijah has his servant urge Ahab to leave before the rain causes his chariot to mire up in the mud.

The curtain comes down on "Act II" of the drama of Elijah and the drought with the heavens black with clouds and a mighty rain lashing the countryside as Ahab races toward Jezreel, 25 km. (17 mi.) away. Elijah, grasped by the hand of the LORD (in the power of the Spirit, cf. 2 Kgs. 3:15; Isa. 8:11; Ezek. 1:3; 8:1; 33:22), runs ahead of him (1 Kgs. 18:45-46). Thus ends this eventful day with Elijah in glorious triumph, with Ahab "almost persuaded," and with Israel apparently won back to their true faith.

THEOLOGICAL REFLECTIONS ON 18:1-46

Chapter 18 is one of the most profound commentaries on the First Commandment in the Bible. It corrects the notion that atheism and abandonment of God are the chief forms of the violation of the commandment. More prevalent, more subtle, and more deadly is the practice of worshipping God *and* "Baal." The chapter reveals that a whole people can learn to go limping with two different opinions, hobbling with one foot for "Baal" and one foot for God, oblivious of how ridiculous and impossible their walk in life is. Through rationalization, at which the human heart is incredibly adept, the most contradictory systems of belief, values, and practices can be made to appear compatible, indeed, necessary to each other. For Ahab and Israel the most compelling rationalization must have been that the acceptance of Canaanite religion was in the national self-interest. At that time Phoenicia was prospering and was embarked on colonial expansion that would shortly (841) lead to the founding of Carthage (cf. William F. Albright, "The Role of the Canaanites in the History of Civilization"). Much of the credit for this success would have gone to Baal. Ahab and Israel could reason that it was the modern, progressive thing to do to welcome the gods of their ally, Phoenicia, so that Israel could enjoy the benefits of Baal as well as the LORD.

Chapter 18 contains three paradigmatic responses to the First Commandment. Ahab, while apparently considering himself a loyal follower of the LORD (his sons who succeed him, Ahaziah and Jehoram, have names compounded with Yahweh), is in favor of official recognition and tolerance of Baal and Asherah. Obadiah goes along with official policy but secretly, fearfully, self-righteously, assists the persecuted prophets of the LORD. He calls both Ahab and Elijah "lord" (vv. 7, 10). At great personal risk, Elijah "shows" himself to Ahab (vv. 1, 15) and publicly opposes Canaanite religion as irreconcilable with Israelite religion. Of these positions there can be no doubt as to which one is considered correct. Nowhere in the Bible is it stated more emphatically that there can be no compromise between Baal—in whatever form—and the God of the Bible. And nowhere is it clearer that it is the role of the prophet to identify the threat to true faith in his or her day, especially when it has been made to seem so reasonable and acceptable that most are oblivious to it, and to call their fellow citizens to a decision.

Since Baal is not part of contemporary experience, it is easy to regard Elijah's question and call for decision in v. 21 as having no relevance for us today. But are not the values and practices of Canaanite religion as real now as they were in the time of Elijah? Indeed, does not "Baal" still live? Do not many of us of the industrialized nations tend to look to "Baal" for commercial success (our equivalent of rain), resorting to dishonest practices "in order to survive," and see no conflict in worshipping the God of the Bible on Sunday? Do we not also limp with two opinions and need to be called to decision and commitment to the Father of our Lord, Jesus the Christ?

What is most significant about the contest with the Baal prophets is the criterion of true deity that Elijah sets up. It is not a matter of who has the most impressive mythology and ritual or the most esoteric theology. On these grounds the Baal prophets would have easily won. The acid test as set by Elijah was an act of power in answer to prayer. It is a test at once simple and elemental but central to biblical religion. Without the liberation from Egyptian bondage and the resurrection of Jesus there would be no Judaism or Christianity. And the miraculous recovery from a serious illness, the gift of strength, sight, and purpose to the weak, blind, and lost continue to be hallmarks of biblical religion.

ACT III: ELIJAH AT MT. HOREB (19:1-18)

The Elijah of this passage stands in striking contrast to the Elijah of the preceding chapter. In 1 Kgs. 18 the prophet's energy is boundless and he looms larger than life. He stands alone against the king and the prophets of Baal and prevails. One comes to the end of ch. 18 with the feeling that Elijah is invincible. In 19:1-18, however, Elijah is exhausted, in despair, and in need of correction. How ironic and yet how true to life that Elijah should suffer such a reversal following his greatest triumph.

ELIJAH'S FLIGHT (19:1-3)

The glowing elation with which ch. 18 ends is shattered by the response of Jezebel to Ahab's report of "all that Elijah had done, and how he had slain all the prophets with the sword" (19:1). This was Ahab's great opportunity to take a stand for the LORD. Instead, he passively yields to Jezebel's desire for revenge. She vows on oath to take Elijah's life "by this time tomorrow" (v. 2). It is doubtful, however, that public opinion would have permitted her to fulfill her declared intention. Respecting this constraint, Jezebel expresses deadly intent but sends, not a military guard to arrest Elijah, but a single envoy with a threatening message. The result was all she could have hoped for. Fearing for his life, the stalwart prophet of Mt. Carmel flees to Beer-sheba in Judah. In one decisive stroke Jezebel rids the country of Elijah's troubling presence and brings discredit on the prophet and his God.

ELIJAH AT BEER-SHEBA (19:4-8)

Beer-sheba lay at the southern border of the Promised Land and afforded Elijah a safe refuge. More important than physical security was a spiritual need, for Elijah was in despair. Beer-sheba provided a resource for this need as well. It was the site of a sanctuary founded by Abraham (Gen. 21:33) and a favorite place of pilgrimage to persons of the northern kingdom (Amos 5:5; 8:14).

Despair characteristically seeks space for itself and solitude. Elijah leaves his servant and goes a day's journey into the wilderness. Only then do we learn how acute is his mental anguish. Sitting down under a solitary broom tree, the desert's meager source of shade, he who "went for his life" from Jezebel petitions God that he might die (1 Kgs. 19:4a; cf. Num. 11:15; Jer. 20:14-18; Job 3; Jonah 4:3). Although Elijah wants to die, it does not occur to him to commit suicide. He requests God to take his life because life belongs to God and it is not within the province of humans to dispose of life.

Elijah wants to die because he feels himself to be "no better than [his] fathers" (1 Kgs. 19:4b). The context suggests that Elijah has in mind his prophetic predecessors, his spiritual fathers. If this is correct, Elijah's wish expresses a deep sense of failure. He had thought he would make a difference in the life of Israel, but just as his prophetic forebears had failed, so had he. Physically and psychically exhausted, Elijah seeks escape in sleep.

As Elijah abandons responsibility for himself, an elusive heavenly presence ("an angel," v. 5; LXX "someone") rouses him to food and water miraculously provided and encourages him to eat and drink. Elijah's despair is sweet, and he savors it. He does eat and drink but afterward seeks again the oblivion of sleep (v. 6). A second time he is awakened by "the angel of the LORD," urged to eat, and reminded of a rendezvous he has yet to keep (v. 7). Elijah's despair is so great that the remedy for it must be sought at the most holy place for an Israelite, Mt. Horeb (also called Mt. Sinai), the place where Moses met God at the burning bush, where the Ten Commandments were given, and where Israel plighted her troth to God in covenant—a covenant now forsaken. This time Elijah turns his back to the siren call of self-pity and goes "in the strength of that food forty days and forty nights to Horeb the mount of God" (v. 8). At this fount of Israel's blessing, Elijah seeks solace for his soul.

GOD'S QUESTION AND ELIJAH'S ANSWER (19:9-11a)

At Horeb Elijah finds lodging in "the cave" (v. 9a MT). The definite article implies that the cave was famous or well-known, probably "the cleft of the rock" where Moses witnessed God's presence (Exod. 33:17-23). After an unspecified time the word of the LORD comes to Elijah in the form of a question. Elijah must have had some questions of his own, but God is the first to ask, and his question must have taken the prophet aback: "What are you doing here, Elijah?" (1 Kgs. 19:9b). "Here" (i.e., Horeb) stands in contrast to the land of Israel from which Elijah had fled. There may also be a secondary reference to Elijah being in the cave. In any case, the contrast is between escape and responsibility, and the question is reproving. Elijah is where he has no business to be.

Elijah's answer discloses much about the state of his inner being: "I have been very jealous [*qana'* also means "zealous"] for the LORD, the God of hosts [cf. 18:15]; for the people of Israel have forsaken thy covenant, thrown down thy altars, and slain thy prophets with the sword; and I, even I only, am left; and they seek my life, to take it away" (19:10). Coming as it does after the events on Mt. Carmel, this statement means that Elijah regards his efforts there to have been in vain and the forces of Baal to have been victorious after all.

As a magnet shapes iron filings, so the behavior of a head of state shapes the behavior of the nation. The people's commitment on Mt. Carmel (18:39) is annulled by Ahab's failure to witness to the LORD's victory, by his lack of support for Elijah, and by his yielding to Jezebel. Elijah no longer speaks of Ahab and his father's house as forsaking the LORD's covenant (v. 18) but of the people who do so. It is the people, not Ahab or Jezebel, who throw down the LORD's altars (cf. v. 30), slay the LORD's prophets (cf. vv. 4, 13), and seek Elijah's life (19:1).

Elijah is bitter. He had given his best effort and victory had been within his grasp. One can well imagine what thoughts he must have had about the resistance of the human heart to God and the fickleness of the people who on Mt. Carmel had confessed, "The LORD, he is God; the LORD, he is God." The defeat smote Elijah at the core of his being, calling into question that which gave his life meaning and purpose, his function as a prophet. This is why he wanted to die.

Companion to this profound sense of failure are feelings of self-pity and self-righteousness. Elijah's reference to his zeal for the LORD and to himself as the only loyal one left is a plaintive tribute to himself. It is clear that he expected, not God's question, but a well-done-good-and-faithful-servant commendation and expressions of compassion for his hardship.

God does not respond directly to Elijah but commands the prophet to go forth from the cave and "stand upon the mount before the LORD" (v. 11a).

THE THEOPHANY (19:11b-14)

The divine self-manifestation that follows is one of the most famous in the Bible. The way God chooses to manifest himself is an integral part of the revelation he wishes to communicate. When God reveals himself to Isaiah sitting upon a throne and wearing a royal robe (Isa. 6), it is his kingship he wants to convey. Here the theophany begins in a manner reminiscent of the revelation to Moses and the liberated Israelites (Exod. 19:16-19; 20:18; Deut. 4:11-12; 5:22-26) but ends in an unexpectedly different way.

And, behold, the LORD passed by, and a great and strong wind rent the mountains, and broke in pieces the rocks before the LORD, but the LORD was not in the wind; and after the wind an earthquake, but the LORD was not in the earthquake; and after the earthquake a fire, but the LORD was not in the fire; and after the fire a still small voice. (1 Kgs. 19:11b-12)

Paradoxically, God brings about the wind, earthquake, and fire only to disassociate himself from each. And the disassociation is deliberate and emphatic. God was not "in" the wind, nor "in" the earthquake, nor "in" the fire. The climactic reference to fire points back to God's manifestation of himself on Mt. Carmel (18:38). It suggests that God is concerned to correct the misconception arising from that experience, that he was identical with the cosmic powers of nature or that he could be perceived only through them.

Initially, the theophany is similar to the one experienced by Moses (Exod. 19:16, 18). But instead of the wind, earthquake, and fire culminating in God's thundering his revelation to Elijah as he had to Moses (Exod. 19:19), they are followed by "a still small voice" (1 Kgs. 19:12b), *qol demamah daqqah. Qol* means "voice, sound, noise," depending on the context. *Demamah,* found elsewhere only in Job 4:16 and Ps. 107:29, denotes "calmness, stillness, silence, whisper." *Daqqah* refers to that which has been reduced and made "thin, fine, small." *Daqqah* is not elsewhere used in relation to sound, but may also have the sense of "soft, gentle." Since Elijah hears the *qol demamah daqqah* (1 Kgs. 19:13a), the reference must be to a filled, gripping, perceptible silence or stillness. God is present in it, and his presence is so real that Elijah must cover his face in his mantle.

The still, small voice draws Elijah to the mouth of the cave (v. 13b). In v. 11a God had commanded Elijah to stand before him on the mount. Did Elijah not obey God's command? Or did Elijah obey only to retreat into the cave because of the wind, earthquake, and fire? It has been noted that Moses stood both upon Mt. Horeb/Sinai (Exod. 19:20) and in a cleft of a rock (Exod. 33:21-22), and some scholars think the discrepancy between 1 Kgs. 19:11 and 13 occurs because editors wanted to emphasize the parallel between Moses and Elijah. At the entrance of the cave "behold, there came a voice to him, and said, 'What are you doing here, Elijah?'" (v. 13b).

The repetition of this question confirms that God is concerned to correct a serious misconception on the part of Elijah. Elijah does not perceive it and lamely repeats his answer as before (v. 14).

ELIJAH'S NEW COMMISSION (19:15-18)

God does not press Elijah further but answers the question for him by giving him a new commission. God charges Elijah to return to the world from which he had fled and to anoint Hazael to be king over Syria, Jehu to be king over Israel, and Elisha to be Elijah's successor as prophet. They are to be anointed as instruments of God's judgment, each wielding the sword against Israel in collaboration with the other. "And him who escapes from the sword of Hazael shall Jehu slay; and him who escapes from the sword of Jehu shall Elisha slay" (v. 17). The reason for the judgment, not stated but clear from the context, is the apostasy of Israel. It is also implicit from the context that Hazael, Jehu, and Elisha will accomplish what Elijah was unable to, namely, complete victory over Baalism.

The commission to anoint Hazael, Jehu, and Elisha, then, is an affirmation of Elijah. It means that he had not failed; rather, Ahab and Israel had failed. At Carmel Israel had the opportunity to choose life and blessing. Because of Ahab's indecision they chose the curse and death (Deut. 30:15-20). God's purpose would now be accomplished through judgment.

Judgment is characteristically accompanied by grace in the Bible, and so it is here. God reveals to Elijah that there are seven thousand who have not bowed the knee (cf. 1 Kgs. 8:54) to Baal or kissed him (cf. Hos. 13:2). These God will "leave" *(wehish'arti)* in the coming judgment. Here in germinal form is the idea of the remnant *(she'ar)*, an Israel within Israel, a community identified by its faithfulness and potentially transcending ethnicity and nationality (cf. Rom. 11:1-6).

Elijah's commission was fulfilled, but not exactly as given. It was Elisha, not Elijah, who was responsible for Hazael's becoming king (2 Kgs. 8:7-15). It was also Elisha who through his servant anointed Jehu to be king (2 Kgs. 9:1-10). Hazael did wield the sword against Israel (2 Kgs. 10:32-33), but subsequent to Jehu's bloody purge (9:14–10:27), not before it. Elijah does make Elisha his successor, but there is no mention of anointing or of Elisha's slaying those who escaped from Jehu. Did Elijah's health or some unforeseen circumstance prevent him from carrying out the commission as directed? Anointing seems to be used here in a metaphorical sense (cf. Isa. 45:1; 61:1; Ps. 105:15).

THEOLOGICAL REFLECTIONS ON 19:1-18

It was a major theological breakthrough for Israel, inexperienced as they were in agriculture, to come to the realization that the LORD, not Baal, was the source of fertility. It was a signal achievement on the part of Elijah to bring the nation to this understanding. As a result, however, it appears that Elijah had come to think of the LORD as a bigger and better Baal. As one tends to become like the enemy one opposes, so Elijah's preoccupation with Baal seems to have led him to conceive the LORD in Baal's image. By pointedly disassociating the divine presence from the wind, earthquake, and fire, the LORD's message to Elijah is that, while he is sovereign over the powers felt in nature, he is not "in" any of these; the LORD is no Baal.

The LORD also wants Elijah to understand that the divine presence does not require outward, tangible expressions. It may be manifested imperceptibly and perceived inwardly and spiritually. This is the significance of the still, small voice and the point of the comparison and contrast with the original theophany on Horeb/Sinai. The similar beginning but different ending of the theophany to Elijah means that one does not need external demonstrations and proofs of God's presence. God manifests himself imperceptibly and speaks directly to the human heart. This imperceptible but direct experience of God's presence is a breakthrough in the understanding of the nature of God that prepares the way for the rich spirituality of the prophets and psalmists. And this new mode of God's presence is just as real and powerful as the cosmic forces of nature. This is the meaning of the juxtaposition of the still, small voice with the wind, earthquake, and fire.

Whenever we locate God "in" (i.e., identify God with) our political or economic system, nation, class, race, or denomination, we also conceive God in Baal's image. And whenever we insist that God is to be found only in a certain dogma or interpretation of scripture or style of worship, we need to learn with Elijah that God's manifestation of himself may come as "a still small voice" rather than as "wind, earthquake, or fire."

God's question, "What are you doing here, Elijah?," concerns the proper place and role of a prophet. Because of his victory on Carmel, Elijah seems to think of himself as a lone, heroic figure whose function is to stage dramatic demonstrations of divine power before large convocations of people. The behavior of Ahab and the people after Carmel proves that spectacular demonstrations of divine power do not automatically conquer the human heart. By rebuffing Elijah with his question and by sending him back into the world from which he had fled, God makes it clear to Elijah that the locus of divine activity is in the social arena and that God's purposes are to be implemented by human agents. The proper role of the prophet is to be the instrument of God's purpose in the affairs of everyday life.

Elijah arrives at Horeb with the conviction that no one is as zealous for God as he, that he is the only true servant of God left, that God's cause depends on Elijah's success or failure. The Elijah who seeks refuge at Horeb is also "burned out," in despair, and his ministry seemingly at an end. At Horeb Elijah learns (what many an "Elijah" needs to learn) that despite appearances to the contrary God is in control, that there are "seven thousand" others who are loyal and who share the responsibility for God's cause, that God's timetable may differ from ours, and that the final victory may rest with a future generation and with other leaders God has already chosen.

A recurring structural pattern in 1 Kgs. 17, 18, and 19:1-18 is a conversion experience. In ch. 17 it is the conversion of the widow of Zarephath (17:24), and in ch. 18 the conversion of the people (18:39). While there is no explicit reference to it, 19:1-18 also has to do with a conversion experience—Elijah's. It is attested in the very fact that Elijah made his Horeb experience public. It is an experience of intense and painful self-examination under the searing scrutiny of God. With remarkable candor, Elijah lets himself be seen fearful for his life, wanting to die, self-pitying and self-righteous, seeking to escape into the womb of the past and the cave, and grasping for tangible proof of God's presence and power. Because of his honesty with himself and with God, Elijah is corrected and empowered to return to an active ministry with renewed strength and vision, to choose a successor, and to be content to leave the outcome in God's hands and with a future generation. 1 Kings 19:1-18 is not only an account of a long trek to Beer-sheba and Horeb; it is also witness to a profound inward journey. Through that journey Elijah wins a victory even greater than that on Mt. Carmel.

THE CALL OF ELISHA
1 Kings 19:19-21

The scene shifts abruptly to Abel-meholah, traditionally located in the middle Jordan Valley, where Elijah has come in obedience to God's command to anoint Elisha as his successor. Elijah seeks out a group of men who are plowing, walks silently past eleven of them, and upon the twelfth, Elisha, casts his mantle. Without a word he continues on his way (19:19). By this act, Elijah both tests Elisha's readiness to serve and allows him to respond in freedom.

The mantle, made of hair (2 Kgs. 1:8; Zech. 13:4; Matt. 3:4), was the symbol of the prophetic office (2 Kgs. 2:8, 13-14). Elisha immediately grasps the significance of what Elijah has done and accepts his summons, but asks permission to take leave of his parents (1 Kgs. 19:20a). Elijah's reply is cryptic. Does Elijah disclaim having done anything by casting his mantle so as to place the responsibility for a commitment fully on Elisha (NJV)? Or is the sense elliptical and solicitous: "Go, (but) return, because of what I have done to you"? Whatever the precise meaning, it is clear from the context that Elisha understands that he may follow Elijah and that he may also take leave of his parents (v. 21).

Elisha begins his career as an apprentice, serving as Elijah's attendant. This is the only account in the OT of such an entry into the prophetic office, but it may have been customary at the time (cf. Exod. 24:13; 33:11; Num. 11:28; Josh. 1:1). There is no formal ceremony of anointing, nor was it the practice in the OT to anoint prophets. Elijah must have taken the bestowal of his mantle on Elisha and Elisha's response as the equivalent of anointing.

THEOLOGICAL REFLECTIONS ON 19:19-21

Elisha's summons to be a prophet was a call to an office of risk.

165

Prophets had been killed, others were in hiding (1 Kgs. 18:4, 13), and Jezebel had run Elijah out of the country (19:1-3). The office to which Elisha was called was not a popular one. The prevalent mood was one of accommodation to Canaanite religion (18:21). Nor was prophecy an economically secure calling. Elisha had to give up his life as a farmer (and if the twelve yoke of oxen were his, he was a very wealthy farmer) and follow Elijah. Elisha's call required humility. He who probably was a prosperous farmer had to become Elijah's attendant. Above all, Elijah's summons meant that Elisha had to make a complete break with his old way of life and become totally committed to the new. In spite of all this, Elisha accepted with joy and enthusiasm. He was so honored by Elijah's summons and so eager to accept that he ran after Elijah. And Elisha celebrated his new calling with a sacrificial meal with the people of Abel-meholah and demonstrated his commitment by preparing the meal from the very yoke of oxen with which he had been plowing. Christian discipleship is equally if not more demanding and equally if not more a privilege and a joy (Matt. 8:18-22; Luke 9:57-62; cf. Matt. 19:23-30; Mark 10:23-31).

WAR WITH SYRIA
1 Kings 20:1-43

At Horeb it was revealed to Elijah that Israel must experience judgment at the hands of Hazael, Jehu, and Elisha. Thus far, however, the case against Ahab and Israel has been inconclusive. Elijah made a valiant effort to win the king and nation to the LORD and almost succeeded. A turning point comes when Ahab fails to act decisively on what he witnessed at Mt. Carmel and lets Jezebel drive Elijah out of the country. 1 Kgs. 20 and 21 complete the indictment against Ahab and show cause why the Omri dynasty and Israel must experience the judgment revealed to Elijah at Horeb.

Chapter 20 concerns two battles between Israel and Syria. Center stage is occupied by Ahab, Ben-hadad of Syria, and an unnamed prophet. Elijah does not appear in this chapter. (It is in keeping with his mysterious habits that the prophet's whereabouts should be unknown during these events.) The battles constitute an important chapter in the history of Israel, but they are presented without any mention of the background circumstances, and not enough is known of political history to place them in their proper context with certainty. They are not reported for their own sake, however, but because of the role Ahab played in them and how it affected his status before God. The first battle takes place at Samaria, the second at Aphek, and the chapter concludes with an episode following the battle at Aphek.

THE BATTLE AT SAMARIA (20:1-21)

20:1-12 *The Siege of Samaria.* These verses plunge the reader into the midst of a situation where Israel has been invaded and the capital, Samaria, placed under siege. The aggressor is Ben-hadad, king of Syria, along with thirty-two kings (i.e., petty allies and vassals). Since Ahab addresses Ben-hadad as "my lord" (20:4, 9) and accepts his right to take spoil (vv. 3-4), Israel is apparently the vassal of Syria—a surprising development for which the text provides no explanation. The purpose of this campaign seems not so much military in nature as it is an opportunity for Ben-hadad to assert his authority and to impress his allies and vassals. "Succoth" ("booths") is also the name of a place in the Jordan Valley near the mouth of the Jabbok River. If *succot* is taken as a place name in vv. 12 and 16 (NJV, NEB mg), then Ben-hadad's main camp would have been there and the verbal exchanges that follow would have been carried out by messengers shuttling back and forth.

The action of the opening scene is expressed by three exchanges of messages between Ahab and Ben-hadad. In the first exchange, Ben-hadad asserts his right to the silver, gold, fairest wives, and children of Ahab, presumably as hostages (cf. 2 Kgs. 14:14; 18:15). Ahab verbally acknowledges this claim (1 Kgs. 20:2-4). In the second exchange, Ben-hadad is not content with Ahab's verbal submission and arrogantly escalates his demands, presenting Ahab with an ultimatum. Ahab must literally comply with the Syrian king's demands within twenty-four hours or his officers will enter Samaria and take whatever they please. Supported by the elders of Israel, Ahab refuses (vv. 5-9). In the third exchange, the enraged Ben-hadad threatens on oath (cf. 19:2) to reduce Samaria to rubble. He boasts that his troops are so many that it would be impossible for each one to gather a handful of Samaria's dust (cf. 2 Sam. 17:13). Ahab replies, "Let not him that girds on his armor boast himself as he that puts it off." With this exchange the Syrians prepare for battle (1 Kgs. 20:10-12).

20:13-15 *Prophetic Intervention.* At this juncture an unnamed prophet approaches Ahab and in the name of the LORD assures him of victory that "you shall know that I am the LORD" (v. 13). Upon Ahab's request the prophet also gives the winning strategy: a decoying elite corps of 232 men backed up by 7,000 regular troops (vv. 14-15).

20:16-21 *The Battle.* Adopting the strategy supplied by the prophet, Ahab attacks at noon while the Syrians are carousing and defeats them, but Ben-hadad escapes on horseback.

THE BATTLE AT APHEK (20:22-34)

20:22 *Counsel for Ahab.* Despite Ahab's victory, Ben-hadad's escape means that Israel has not seen the last of the Syrians. The initiative in dealing with this eventuality is taken by "the prophet," that is, the one instrumental in Ahab's victory (v. 13), who counsels Ahab to prepare for the Syrians to resume hostilities the following spring.

20:23-25 *Counsel for Ben-hadad.* Ben-hadad's "servants" (not prophets) advise him that he can regain control over Israel by choosing a battle site in the plain, by replacing the kings with "commanders" (i.e., professional soldiers), and by bringing his army back to full strength and reequipping it. If the engagement at Samaria was essentially political, this time it is to be strictly military. The choice of the site is the crucial element, for the Syrian advisors account for their defeat on the assumption that the "gods" of the Israelites (from their polytheistic point of view) are "gods of the hills" (v. 23) and are superior there but at a disadvantage in the valleys (v. 28).

20:26-30a *The Battle.* His army reorganized and reequipped, Ben-hadad invades Israel in the spring, but this time takes up a position at Aphek. The OT records five different cities named Aphek. The most likely one in this context is located at modern Fiq near the southern end of the Sea of Galilee. Mustered to oppose Ben-hadad, the forces of Israel were like "two little flocks of goats, but the Syrians filled the country" (v. 27). Again, a "man of God" (presumably the prophet of vv. 13, 22) intervenes and proclaims victory for Israel "because the Syrians have said, 'The LORD is a god of the hills but he is not a god of the valleys,'" and in order that Ahab may know "that I am the LORD" (v. 28). After seven days the battle is joined, and Israel routs the Syrians. When those who survive the battle flee into Aphek the wall falls on them and kills them (vv. 29-30; cf. Josh. 6:12-21).

20:30b-34 *The Sparing of Ben-hadad.* This time Ben-hadad does not escape but seeks refuge in "an inner chamber" at Aphek. His officers, who have heard that "the kings of the house of Israel are merciful kings," advise Ben-hadad to give himself up to Ahab and appeal for mercy. As at the beginning of the passage, the two monarchs negotiate, but this time their positions are reversed. To the surprise of the Syrians, Ahab treats Ben-hadad graciously. He ignores Ben-hadad's designation of himself as "servant," calls him "brother," invites the Syrian king to join him in his chariot, and there negotiates a settlement. Ben-hadad agrees to restore the cities his father had taken from Ahab's father and grants Ahab the right to establish bazaars in Damascus as his father had done in Samaria (cf. Neh. 13:16). On these conditions they make a covenant, and Ben-hadad is released.

THE CASE OF THE ESCAPED PRISONER (20:35-43)

One comes to the end of the account of the battle at Aphek with a feeling of satisfaction and completion. Samaria has been saved and the Syrians decisively defeated. And Ahab seems to have redeemed himself. He accepted with dignity his subservience to Ben-hadad but was not obsequious. He consulted the elders of Israel and acted with their support. He heeded the words of the anonymous prophet and, adopting his strategy, was victorious. And he was magnanimous in his treatment of Ben-hadad. 1 Kgs. 20:35-43, which deals in parabolic fashion with the case of an escaped prisoner, seems at first like an appendix to the preceding, but these verses are full of surprises and provide the interpretive key to the entire chapter.

20:35-38 *The Prophet's Disguise.* This episode belongs to the aftermath of the battle of Aphek. It involves wounded soldiers, responsibility for prisoners, and Ahab's release of Ben-hadad, but it is not identified in terms of time and place. In the first scene, a "man of the sons of the prophets" (i.e., a member of a prophetic guild) wants someone to strike him hard enough to wound him but does not explain why. The first person he asks, a fellow prophet, refuses, only to learn that he has disobeyed the voice of the LORD and has incurred the penalty of death by a lion (cf. 13:20-25). When a second person complies with the prophet's demand, the prophet bandages his eyes, pretending to be a wounded soldier, and stations himself by the side of the road to wait for the king. The mystery of this strange behavior is heightened by the prophet's concern to conceal his identity, for the bandage also serves as a disguise. If the prophet is the same person as in 20:13, 22, 28, as seems likely, he would have been known to Ahab. Possibly he would also have borne a mark of some kind on his forehead that would have identified him as a prophet (v. 41; cf. Ezek. 9:4).

20:39-43 *The Parable of the Escaped Prisoner.* In a third scene where people, including the king, are coming and going on a road near a battlefield, the disguised prophet appeals to Ahab to settle his case. The prophet says he had been charged to keep a prisoner on the condition that "if by any means he be missing, your life shall be for his life, or else you shall pay a talent of silver" (1 Kgs. 20:39). A talent of silver was one hundred times the price of a slave (Exod. 21:32) and well beyond the means of an ordinary soldier. The penalty is surprisingly stiff and implies that the prisoner was someone of extraordinary importance or that it was deliberately excessive in order to enforce vigilance. The prophet, clearly hoping for mercy, confesses that because he was "busy here and there" the prisoner escaped (1 Kgs. 20:40).

Acting in his capacity as the highest legal authority of the realm (cf. 3:16-28; 2 Kgs. 6:26-31; 8:3-6), Ahab rules, "So shall your judgment be; you yourself have decided it" (1 Kgs. 20:40). But in deciding the case Ahab has passed judgment on himself. The prophet removes his bandage, disclosing his identity. He designates Ahab as "the man" (cf. 2 Sam. 12:7) and declares that Ahab has acted just as irresponsibly as the caretaker of the prisoner in letting Ben-hadad, whom God had devoted to destruction, go free. Ahab's penalty is this: "Your life shall go for his life, and your people for his people" (1 Kgs. 20:42). The death of the person who refused to strike the prophet places a seal of ominous finality on the verdict. Ahab sullenly accepts the judgment against him and returns to Samaria (v. 43).

THEOLOGICAL REFLECTIONS ON 20:1-43

From one point of view, Ahab's treatment of Ben-hadad was generous and humane, especially when compared to the way

Ben-hadad had intended to treat him. Politically and commercially it was also astute. At this time Assyria, the emerging superpower of the biblical world, was beginning to make a sustained effort to gain control of Palestine-Syria. The only possibility for the small Syro-Palestinian states to oppose this threat successfully was by collective action. From Ahab's point of view, a strong, friendly Syria was in Israel's self-interest as an ally and a buffer against Assyria. Not least of all, the right to maintain bazaars in Damascus, a major emporium of the biblical world, would have been a lucrative source of revenue.

The prophet judged Ahab's actions from a fundamentally different perspective, for the prophet was rooted in the holy war traditions of the tribal confederacy, according to which God intervened to give his covenant people victory when they were unjustly threatened. Victory gained in this way was not to be used for material gain or political advantage but that the people might know God, have faith, and give praise. An established practice of warfare so understood was the sacramental "devotion to the LORD for destruction" of the spoil and certain personages (cf. Deut. 7:2; 20:16-18; Josh. 6:15-21; 7; 1 Sam. 15).

The prophet's condemnation places Ahab's behavior in a new light. Ahab did not seek divine guidance before either battle. Nor did he heed the prophet's counsel to prepare for the return of the Syrians, for Israel was woefully unprepared at Aphek. And Ahab completely ignored the transcendent dimension of the victories and the holy war traditions of Israel. Victories against great odds announced beforehand by a prophet for theological purposes are not ordinary victories. The striking parallels to the conquest of Jericho, as the interval of seven days before the battle and the falling of the city walls, clearly identified the battles at Samaria and Aphek as holy war. The examples of Achan (Josh. 7) and Saul (1 Sam. 15) would have been reminders of the importance of treating the spoil and captives as sacrosanct. Incredibly, Ahab treated the victories at Samaria and Aphek as his own achievement. In violation of the demands of holy war, Ahab kept and used the horses and chariots of the Syrians (1 Kgs. 20:21). Worst of all, he spared Ben-hadad. The appropriate time to have shown mercy was to the "wounded" soldier. Ahab let Ben-hadad go solely to gain political and commercial advantage. Ahab's behavior is all the more damaging because his forces were so obviously inadequate and because divine intervention came not once but twice.

Whenever we favor and release a "Ben-hadad" but condemn without mercy a "common soldier," whenever we relinquish an important standard or principle for cheap, self-serving mercy— especially after God has richly blessed us—we follow in the footsteps of Ahab.

What is it that the LORD wanted Ahab to know through the victories at Samaria and Aphek (vv. 13, 28)? The context is the interpretive guide. The king and Israel faced an impossible situation. Of their own resources they had no chance against the superior forces of the Syrians. Yet precisely in these circumstances the prophet proclaimed victory "that you may know that I am the LORD"—the one who does the unexpected and the unthinkable, who grants victory against all expectations and seemingly impossible odds.

Additional depth is given to this revelation by the LORD's refusal to be identified as a god of the hills (v. 28). Just as God disassociates himself from the wind, earthquake, and fire (ch. 19), so also he refuses to be localized or confined to the hills. As God is sovereign both over history and fertility (ch. 18), so he is God both of the "hills" and the "valleys." These affirmations are metaphorical ways of saying that God is spirit and free of all the constraints we are wont to place upon him.

This chapter has much in common with ch. 13 in its emphasis on strict obedience. Both the man of God from Judah (ch. 13) and Ahab have many admirable qualities, but in the end both are condemned because they were not perfect in obedience. Perfect obedience requires alertness and vigilance. The Judahite prophet accepted too readily the Bethelite prophet's claim to have received a revelation (13:18-19). Ahab ignored clue upon clue that the battles at Samaria and Aphek were holy wars. And the soldier lost the prisoner entrusted to him because he was "busy here and there" (20:40). The passage calls for obedience even when the demand may not make sense at the time. This is the point of the tragic end of the prophet who refused to strike his colleague (vv. 35-36). There is no middle ground for casual obedience or self-serving mercy. Anything less than complete obedience is disobedience, and the consequences can be death.

Chapter 20 begins with Ahab enjoying God's favor and ends with him a condemned man. What transpires here is not an isolated happening but a climactic development in a long process. Ahab had walked in the sins of Jeroboam, supported and participated in the worship of Baal and Asherah (16:29-33), and sanctioned the rebuilding of Jericho although it was prohibited by a curse (v. 34). Moreover, he rejected two powerful interventions by prophets to show him the folly of his ways: the vindication of God on Mt. Carmel (ch. 18) and the miraculous victories over the Syrians (20:1-34). That the victories at Samaria and Aphek are given explicitly that Ahab might know the true nature of the LORD is a final appeal to the king. Ahab spurned that appeal, and by the power of his influence as king he also condemned his people. This is why Ahab and Israel must experience judgment and why Elijah was commissioned to anoint Hazael, Ben-hadad's successor, to be the instrument of that judgment.

The road to Ahab's condemnation was a long one. Despite Ahab's many sins, it is only at this point that judgment is pronounced on him. It is not God's judgment but his grace and mercy that are noteworthy in his treatment of Ahab.

NABOTH'S VINEYARD
1 Kings 21:1-29

For anyone concerned about social justice, this chapter is required reading. Its theme is the abuse of authority by the powerful against the weak—a king and queen with all the resources of the state at their disposal arrayed against a small farmer! While Elijah plays an important role, the focus of attention is not on him but on Naboth's case. As if presenting evidence before a court of law, the narrator with restrained outrage—but not without compassion—recounts events factually, clearly assigns motive and guilt, and invites the reader to sit as jury.

AHAB'S OFFER AND NABOTH'S REFUSAL (21:1-4)

It is well known from both the biblical text (16:34; 22:39) and archaeological excavations at Samaria, Megiddo, and Hazor that Ahab was a great builder. Among his many holdings was a palace at Jezreel that seems to have been a favorite retreat for the king and his family. Ahab and Jezebel were in residence there at the time of the contest on Mt. Carmel (18:46). It was there that Joram, Ahab's son, returned to recuperate after being wounded at Ramoth-gilead (2 Kgs. 8:29; 9:15). Also, Jezebel apparently preferred Jezreel as her residence after the death of Ahab (2 Kgs. 9:30-37).

One explanation for this fondness for Jezreel is that Ahab's ancestral home was there and it was a place to be in touch with his roots. Another possibility is that because it is 305 m. (1,000 ft.) lower in elevation and therefore warmer than Samaria, Jezreel may have been a winter residence, an expression of luxury and indulgence. No charge is brought against Ahab for having this dwelling, whatever its nature and purpose, but he is held accountable for the way he treats his neighbor.

Adjacent to Ahab's palace in Jezreel is a vineyard owned by Naboth that the king wants for a vegetable garden. One day Ahab calls on Naboth and makes a fair if not generous offer: a better vineyard in exchange or its value in money (1 Kgs. 21:2). To Ahab's surprise and chagrin Naboth refuses, exclaiming, "The LORD forbid [literally, 'a profanation to me from the LORD'] that I should give you the inheritance of my fathers" (v. 3). Ahab accepts Naboth's refusal but goes home "vexed and sullen. . . . And he lay down on his bed, and turned away his face, and would eat no food" (v. 4)—just as we would expect of Ahab! (20:43).

Naboth claimed the right to keep his vineyard because it was the inheritance *(nahalah)* of his ancestors. Land was not a private possession and commercial commodity in Israel but a gift and trust held from God, the real owner (Lev. 25:23), for the sake of the family (Num. 27:1-11; 36:1-12). The vineyard was an indulgence to Ahab, but to Naboth it was his link with his ancestors, the source of his identity, livelihood, and position in the community. Here were his roots, and because of his ownership of this land he enjoyed the rights and privileges of a free citizen. Moreover, in the Israelite tradition of kingship the individual had rights even the king was obliged to respect. This is why Ahab did not seize Naboth's property by force in the first place and why he grudgingly accepted Naboth's refusal.

JEZEBEL'S SCHEME (21:5-10)

The scene shifts now to Ahab's private quarters in his palace either at Jezreel or Samaria. Missing him at the dinner table, Jezebel seeks him out to find out what is wrong. Ahab recounts his failure to obtain Naboth's vineyard but does not tell the full story. He does not mention the reason for Naboth's refusal but only quotes him as saying, "I will not give you my vineyard" (1 Kgs. 21:6; cf. v. 15; Naboth had called it his inheritance, *nahalah*). Once Jezebel learns the cause of Ahab's pouting, she knows exactly how to deal with it. She chides him for not asserting his prerogatives as king and promises in a vague, mysterious way to "give" him Naboth's vineyard (vv. 5-7).

If Jezebel knows the Israelite tradition of land ownership, she dismisses it. She is rooted in another set of values, not only of land ownership but of kingship. Her plan is to get Naboth's vineyard through a legal frame-up cloaked in piety. She composes a letter in Ahab's name, signs it with his seal, and sends it to the elders and nobles of Jezreel, instructing them to proclaim a fast and "set Naboth on high among the people." Two "base fellows" are to be seated opposite him, and are to "bring a charge against him, saying, 'You have cursed God and the king.'" Then they shall take Naboth out and stone him to death (vv. 9-10). Could Jezebel count on the complicity of these groups because of a sense of indebtedness created by favors and privileges granted by Omri and Ahab (and family ties)? The nobles in particular were a privileged class that would have owed their position and wealth to the royal family. And the economic advantages of the royal presence would have exerted powerful pressure on all the citizens of Jezreel to approve royal behavior.

Jezebel's scheme reveals that she was well informed about Israelite psychology and legal practice. A fast was called as a result of some misfortune, such as defeat in battle, drought, a plague of locusts, interpreted to be due to God's displeasure (e.g., Judg. 20:26; 1 Sam. 7:6; 2 Chr. 20:1-4; Jer. 36:9; Joel 1:14; Jonah 3:5). The purpose of the fast was to summon the community to repentance, to learn wherein God was displeased, to implore divine mercy, and to make amends. A fast thus created a setting and atmosphere that made it easy to carry out Jezebel's plot by identifying Naboth as the culprit responsible for the calamity (not specified in the text) that made the fast necessary. By setting Naboth in a prominent position or place of honor, possibly in an official capacity (literally, "at the head of the people"), it was easy to make him a target.

To curse God and the king, God's "son" (Ps. 2:7), was blasphemy and punishable by death according to Israel's legal tradition (Exod. 22:28; Lev. 24:10-16). Israelite tradition also required the evidence of two witnesses to pass sentence (Deut. 17:6; 19:15; John 8:17; cf. Num. 35:30; Matt. 26:60). The text does not tell us how the charge of blasphemy was formulated. Presumably the two "scoundrels" (NIV) distorted Naboth's adjuration by the LORD when he refused Ahab's offer (1 Kgs. 21:3).

THE EXECUTION OF JEZEBEL'S SCHEME (21:11-16)

The elders and nobles cooperate fully, a shocking commentary on the morality of the responsible leaders and authorities of Jezreel. Worse still, Naboth's fellow citizens approve the verdict.

To purge the evil of Naboth's alleged crime from their midst, the people of Jezreel take him outside the city to avoid defiling it (Lev. 24:14; Num. 15:36) and execute him by stoning (1 Kgs. 21:13). Moreover, Naboth was subjected to the indignity in death of having his blood licked up by dogs (v. 19). Compounding this dastardly deed, Naboth's sons were also stoned to death (2 Kgs. 9:26). The execution of Naboth's sons could have been justified on the principle of corporate guilt, as in the case of Achan and his family (Josh. 7:22-26; cf. Num. 16:25-33; 2 Sam. 21:6, 9; Esth. 9:13; Dan. 6:24). The real reason would have been to remove all claims to the property. With the removal of Naboth's heirs, the crown assumed the legal right to confiscate Naboth's vineyard (cf. 2 Sam. 9:7; 16:4; 19:29; 2 Kgs. 8:3). God's reproving question to Ahab in 1 Kgs. 21:19, "Have you killed, and also taken possession?" implies that such a practice was contrary to the divine will (cf. Isa. 5:8-10; Mic. 2:1-5). No such right is granted in the legislation of the OT.

Having carried out her instructions, the elders and nobles of Jezreel send word to Jezebel that Naboth has been executed by stoning (1 Kgs. 21:14). Pleased with herself, Jezebel tells Ahab that Naboth's vineyard is his for the taking, "for Naboth is not alive, but dead" (v. 15). Ahab asks no question and makes no protest. Like a spoiled child who has been denied a toy, "as soon as Ahab heard that Naboth was dead, Ahab arose to go down to the vineyard of Naboth the Jezreelite, to take possession of it" (v. 16).

JUDGMENT (21:17-26)

As this story begins at Naboth's vineyard, so it ends there. The word of the LORD comes to Elijah, charging him to meet Ahab there with a weighty word of judgment. Just as Ahab is about to satisfy his covetous desire and the triumph of injustice seems certain, Elijah bursts upon the scene (as was his wont). What a jarring note his presence must have been. Ahab asks with surly resentment: "Have you found me, O my enemy?" (v. 20; cf. 18:17). Elijah responds affirmatively and without further ado pronounces judgment upon the king.

Prophetic announcements of judgment have a regular pattern consisting of the reason (or reasons) for the judgment, the announcement and description of the judgment, and a formula identifying the message as the word of the LORD. This pattern has been disrupted in the present passage by editorial elaborations in Deuteronomic language so as to present a summation of the case against Ahab.

The reasons for the judgment against Ahab are many. In addition to the crime against Naboth in which he broke the commandments against murder, coveting, and theft (21:19a), Ahab sold (enslaved) himself to do "what is evil in the sight of the LORD" (v. 20b), provoked the LORD to anger, and made Israel to sin (v. 22b). The murder of Naboth and expropriation of his property, all the more flagrant after Ahab's other sins and the rejected opportunities at Carmel (ch. 18), Samaria, and Aphek (ch. 20), complete the indictments against Ahab and provide the clinching reason why Jehu should be anointed to displace Ahab and his dynasty (19:16).

The judgment is that Ahab is to suffer a similar fate to that of Naboth (21:19b) and that his dynasty, like those of Jeroboam and Baasha, is to be completely cut off (vv. 21-22a, 24; note the similarity of language to the announcements of judgment against Jeroboam, 14:10-11, and Baasha, 16:2, 4). Jezebel is singled out for special mention in 21:23. Her corpse is to be destroyed and thus denied proper burial, a particularly disturbing prospect to the ancient mind. Verses 25-26 give a summary theological evaluation of Ahab, emphasizing that he was the chief of sinners among Israel's kings and that his most serious offense was going after idols in the "Amorite" (another word for "Canaanite") manner (cf. 16:30-33).

GRACE (21:27-29)

God's final word to Ahab is not one of judgment but of grace. This time Ahab repents. "And when Ahab heard those words, he rent his clothes, and put sackcloth upon his flesh, and fasted and lay in sackcloth and went about dejectedly" (21:27). Because of this, God in a private communication to Elijah postpones the end of Ahab's dynasty into the next generation (vv. 28-29).

THEOLOGICAL REFLECTIONS ON 21:1-29

The crime of Ahab and Jezebel begins in covetousness, and all the terrible things that follow grow out of this sin. The story affirms that covetousness cannot be justified even for a king by right of his office. Nor do the great and powerful have a right to the inheritance of the weak and vulnerable because it is "beside" their "palace," business, or national boundary. There is no more illuminating statement in the Bible on the sin of covetousness than this story.

This narrative subjects the crime of Ahab and Jezebel to powerful scrutiny and strips it of all acceptability. It is not regarded as a statistic, as an unfortunate tragedy one must expect and allow for, but as an abhorrent, intolerable offense that rises up to heaven as a stench in God's nostrils. The guise of piety and legality with which Jezebel cloaks her abuse of power is stripped away, and her deed is exposed in all its arrogance and ruthlessness. Her behavior, the fruit of Canaanite religion, exemplifies the true nature of that religion and accounts for the revulsion with which it is regarded in the OT.

An even greater offense, because of his office, is Ahab's passive acquiescence in Jezebel's deed. While Ahab was not directly involved, there is no question of his guilt (v. 19). His primary responsibility as king was to maintain justice and righteousness, peace and well-being for his subjects, especially the weak and defenseless. Instead, he abandons his duty for selfish gratification.

The responsible authorities of Jezreel and Naboth's neighbors are also collaborators in this "legal" murder. Their consent is telling evidence of the debilitating influence of Canaanite religion and values on the general populace. When the First Commandment is not honored the other commandments suffer. Canaanite influence also contributed to economic injustice. Mic. 6:9-16 refers to "the man with wicked scales" and "rich men . . . full of violence" as the legacy of Omri and Ahab.

The passage is a powerful condemnation of evil, but it is not without compassion. Sin makes God angry (1 Kgs. 21:22), but God is quick to respond to penitence, even that of an arch sinner like Ahab.

Finally, a word of appreciation is due the narrator and redactors who shaped the story so skillfully. Because of them Naboth's death is not in vain. The story of Naboth warns against the use of piety and legality to cloak injustice. It teaches that those who support the plots of a Jezebel, whether by silent acquiescence or overt complicity, share her crime. It is a resounding affirmation that injustice touches God, that "as you did it to one of the least of these my brethren, you did it to me" (Matt. 25:40, 45), that in the cosmic order of things there is a power at work that makes for justice. And the story attests that there is awesome power in the conscience and protest of the individual servant of God.

THE CAMPAIGN TO RECLAIM
RAMOTH-GILEAD

1 Kings 22:1-38

This passage is a companion piece to 1 Kgs. 20. It takes up the story of relations between Israel and Syria after Ahab's victory at Aphek and recounts Ahab's expedition to reclaim Ramoth-gilead, one of the cities the Syrians had promised to return but had failed to do so. The Syrians are clearly at fault. Ahab's cause is just. Moreover, Ahab had won victories over Syria in the past. Would he, a man now under judgment (chs. 20, 21), succeed this time also? The story is full of unexpected twists and turns and keeps the reader in suspense until the end.

THE DECISION TO GO TO WAR TO RECOVER RAMOTH-GILEAD (22:1-4)

The events of these verses are dated three years after Ahab's victory over Ben-hadad at Aphek. The Syrian king (not named) has not made good on his agreement to return the cities that his father had taken from Ahab's father (20:34), in particular Ramoth-gilead, a strategically located city E of the Jordan on the border between Israel and Syria. His patience exhausted, Ahab determines to redress this grievance and summons his chief officials as well as Jehoshaphat, king of Judah, to a conference. Ahab arouses patriotic fervor among his officials by reminding them that Ramoth-gilead belongs to "us" and chides them for accepting things as they are. Then Ahab asks for and secures the agreement of Jehoshaphat to join him in a military expedition against the Syrians at Ramoth-gilead.

The alliance between Ahab and Jehoshaphat is the fruit of the policies initiated by Omri (see above on 16:23-28). Whereas Jehoshaphat's father, Asa, had been at war with Israel and had appealed to Syria for help (15:16-22), Israel and Judah are now allies and the common enemy is Syria. The dominant party in the alliance, as is clear from the present passage, is Israel.

Ahab is regularly designated as "the king of Israel" or "the king" and called by name only once (22:20). It is assumed that the reader knows him from the context and from the fact that Jehoshaphat was his contemporary (v. 41). The setting, which is Samaria (v. 10), is also assumed.

Consultation of Prophets concerning the Campaign (22:5-28)

It was established practice for a ruler to seek guidance or for a priest or prophet to volunteer an oracle before going into battle (e.g., Judg. 4:12-16; 20:27-28; 1 Sam. 14:36-37; 23:1-5; 30:7-8; 2 Sam. 5:19; 1 Kgs. 20:13, 28). Normally, the response to such consultations is unambiguous, but here two conflicting messages are given. This unexpected development disrupts Ahab's plans and claims our attention for most of the remainder of the passage.

22:5-12 *The Oracle of the Four Hundred Prophets.* Although Ahab had experienced two miraculous victories over the Syrians through the agency of a prophet (ch. 20), it is Jehoshaphat who takes the initiative to inquire God's will before going into battle (22:5; cf. 2 Kgs. 3:11). Surprisingly, Ahab is able to summon four hundred prophets. This is a far cry from the situation in 1 Kgs. 18, where the prophets of the LORD are persecuted by Jezebel and are in hiding. But the change reflected here is not all gain. There are now two kinds of prophets: the prophets of Ahab (22:22, 23) and the prophets of the LORD. The prophets of Ahab are yes-men. When Ahab asks, "Shall I [note his dominant role] go to battle against Ramoth-gilead, or shall I forbear?" they answer with one voice, "Go up; for the LORD will give it into the hand of the king" (v. 6).

For some reason Jehoshaphat is not satisfied and asks if there is not "another prophet of the LORD of whom we may inquire?" (v. 7; the four hundred are simply called "prophets," v. 6). There is, a certain Micaiah, the son of Imlah, but Ahab hates him because he never prophesies good concerning him, but evil (v. 8). Jehoshaphat is sympathetic but insistent, and to placate him Ahab sends an officer to fetch Micaiah (v. 9). Jehoshaphat's hesitancy with regard to the oracle of the four hundred prophets incites them to renewed activity. While the two kings wait for Micaiah at the entrance to Samaria, the four hundred prophets prophesy before them. A certain Zedekiah acts out the victory at Ramoth-gilead with horns of iron (symbols of power) and proclaims in the name of the LORD, "With these [horns] you shall push the Syrians until they are destroyed" (v. 11; cf. Deut. 33:17). Such symbolic acts were thought to be especially efficacious, setting the enacted event on its way to becoming reality. Zedekiah's symbolic act is reinforced by his colleagues, who reiterate the original assurance of victory with an emphatic promise of triumph: "Go up to Ramoth-gilead and triumph; the LORD will give it into the hand of the king" (1 Kgs. 22:12; cf. v. 6).

22:13-16 *Micaiah's Surprising Oracle.* The official sent to summon Micaiah informs him of the support of the four hundred prophets for the campaign against Ramoth-gilead and urges him to be cooperative (v. 13). Micaiah replies, "As the LORD lives, what the LORD says to me, that I will speak" (v. 14). But when Ahab consults Micaiah, he answers exactly as the four hundred prophets (v. 15)! It is clear, however, whether by the tone of Micaiah's voice or his nonverbal behavior, that his word is not genuine. He takes the king by surprise in order to gain his attention. To Ahab's credit he insists that Micaiah speak the truth in the name of the LORD (v. 16). (Micaiah's initial message was not so given.) Micaiah then proclaims two visionary experiences.

22:17-18 *Micaiah's First Vision.* In the first vision, Micaiah reports that he "saw all Israel scattered upon the mountains, as sheep that have no shepherd" (v. 17a). This is a clear allusion to defeat and the death of the king, for in the biblical world shepherd was a standing image for the king (e.g., 2 Sam. 5:2; Ezek. 34: Zech. 13:7). An interpretive word of the LORD makes this meaning certain: "These have no master; let each return to his home in peace" (1 Kgs. 22:17b). Ahab's I-told-you-so to Jehoshaphat indicates that he understands the unfavorable import

of the vision (v. 18). Ahab seems more concerned to prove that
he was right about Micaiah than he is with the prophecy itself.

22:19-23 *Micaiah's Second Vision.* Anticipating the question
raised by the conflict between his vision and the oracle of the four
hundred prophets, Micaiah recounts a second vision (vv. 19b-22;
cf. Isa. 6). Ahab is now named by name (for the only time), and
it is made explicit that he will lose his life if he attacks Ramoth-
gilead. The reason the four hundred prophets prophesied victory
was because God sent a "lying spirit" into them to entice Ahab
to his fate (more on this later). In 1 Kgs. 22:23 Micaiah sums up
the meaning of what he has seen, which is the word of the LORD
to Ahab (v. 19a): "Now therefore behold, the LORD has put a
lying spirit in the mouth of all these your prophets; the LORD has
spoken evil concerning you."

22:24-28 *The Reaction to Micaiah's Prophecy.* Micaiah's defeatist
prophecy rests ill with those determined to do battle. The first to
oppose it is another prophet, Zedekiah. He strikes Micaiah on the
cheek and asks angrily, "How did the Spirit of the LORD go from
me to speak to you?"—clear evidence that Zedekiah believed
himself to be divinely inspired. Ahab has Micaiah imprisoned and
placed on a scant diet (vv. 26-27). Micaiah affirms to both
Zedekiah and Ahab that events will confirm the truth of his
prophecy, the classic test of a true prophet (Deut. 18:21-22; Jer.
28:8-9).

THE BATTLE AT RAMOTH-GILEAD (22:29-38)

Defying Micaiah, Ahab and Jehoshaphat go to war to reclaim
Ramoth-gilead. To outwit any ill fortune, Ahab disguises himself
as an ordinary soldier but insists that Jehoshaphat wear his royal
robes. The Syrians, intent on capturing Ahab, mistake Jehoshaphat
for the Israelite king, but Jehoshaphat "cried out," making clear his
identity, and was spared. So far so good. Just then the question that
has gripped the reader all along is finally answered. "A certain man
drew his bow at a venture, and struck the king of Israel between
the scale armor and the breastplate" (1 Kgs. 22:34).

Although seriously wounded, Ahab does not desert the field of battle but has himself propped up in his chariot so that he faces the Syrians. There he remains as the battle rages, all the while his lifeblood ebbing away, until at evening he dies. Upon the news of his death, his troops flee for home.

When Ahab's chariot is washed by the pool of Samaria, dogs lick up his blood "according to the word of the LORD which he had spoken" by Elijah (21:19b). Elijah had specified that this was to happen "in the place where dogs licked up the blood of Naboth," that is, at Naboth's vineyard in Jezreel. As is often the case, the fulfillment of prophecy is not mechanical. Indirectly the prophecy was fulfilled in that the corpse of Ahab's son Joram was cast on the plot of ground belonging to Naboth (2 Kgs. 9:21-26). Because of the OT conception of the solidarity of the family, Ahab in a sense shared in the fate of his son. In an additional indignity to Ahab, harlots washed in the blood-stained waters of the pool of Samaria, probably in the superstitious hope of enhancing their beauty and vitality through contact with royal blood.

THEOLOGICAL REFLECTIONS ON 22:1-38

This passage affords a revealing look at the early prophetic movement in Israel. The most obvious fact about it is that it is not unified. The majority of prophets have been captured by the state and made the servants of its purposes. The four hundred prophets are Ahab's prophets (1 Kgs. 22:22, 23). But there is a small minority, including Elijah, the anonymous prophet of ch. 20, and Micaiah, who maintain their independence and speak only what God bids them to speak. This cleavage was to remain throughout the history of prophecy. While the state has legitimate interests that may be supported, the true prophet maintains a certain distance from it. It is only from this stance, freed from the self-interest of the state, that the true prophet is able to bring a transcendent criticism to bear on society.

This passage also discloses that the secret of the true prophet's authority and power is participation in God's council. The divine council is a concept to be found throughout the OT. At the New Year and on special occasions God was thought to meet in formal session with the heavenly host (Job 1:6-12; 2:1-6; 15:8; Ps. 82:1; Dan. 7:9-10; cf. Gen. 1:26; 3:22; 11:7; Exod. 15:11; Ps. 89:5-7;

103:20-21; Isa. 6:8; 40:1-11; Luke 2:13-14). It is the divine assembly in action that Micaiah witnesses in his second vision (1 Kgs. 22:19b-22).

The true prophet represents and acts on behalf of the heavenly council. When Isaiah hears God asking, "Whom shall I send, and who will go for us?" (Isa. 6:8), the "us" are members of the divine council. Participation in the heavenly council was the basis of the unique spirituality of the prophet. Through this experience the prophet was enabled to see as with God's eyes and to feel as with God's heart. The false prophet has not "stood in the council of the LORD" (Jer. 23:18, 22; cf. Abraham J. Heschel, *The Prophets,* ch. 1).

Micaiah's explanation that the deceptive word of the four hundred prophets came from a lying spirit sent by the LORD raises some difficult questions. This is not the only example of this way of thinking in the OT. References to God hardening the human heart (e.g., Exod. 4:21; Deut. 2:30; Ps. 105:25; Isa. 6:9-10) are of a piece with it. Other instances of the divine deception of a prophet are found in Jer. 20:7 and Ezek. 14:9 (cf. 1 Sam. 2:22-25; 2 Sam. 17:14; 24:1; Jer. 4:10; 2 Thess. 2:11-12; 1 John 4:1). The division between Abimelech and the men of Shechem (Judg. 9:23; cf. Judg. 14:4; Isa. 19:2, 14) and the abnormal behavior of Saul are attributed to an evil spirit sent from God (1 Sam. 16:14-16; 18:10). Amos asks, "Does evil befall a city, unless the LORD has done it?" (Amos 3:6). And God declares in Isa. 45:7,

> I form light and create darkness,
>   I make weal and create woe,
>   I am the LORD, who do all these things. (cf. Deut.
> 32:39; 1 Sam. 2:6; 1 Kgs. 17:20; Job 2:10; Lam. 3:38;
> Hos. 6:2-3)

The passages cited above have a common theology that attributes all that happens directly to God. Significantly, the statement in Isa. 45:7 is preceded by the affirmation, "I am the LORD, and there is no other." The concept of Satan as ruler of a kingdom of evil in the NT is not found in the OT. The serpent in Gen. 3 is one of God's creatures (Gen. 3:1), and Satan in Job 1–2 can do only what God permits him to do (Job 1:12; 2:6).

Given the theological presupposition of Micaiah, his explanation makes sense. It was the assurance of the four hundred prophets, spoken sincerely, that emboldened Ahab to place himself in the very situation where the judgment pronounced against him could be realized. If one takes as seriously as Micaiah that God is the fundamental cause of all that happens, it is not difficult to see God's hand at work even in misguided sincerity.

The behavior of Ahab in 1 Kgs. 22:1-38 is another striking example of the incredible obduracy of the human heart (cf. Jeroboam in ch. 13). Ahab had witnessed the miracle at Carmel, experienced divine intervention at Samaria and Aphek, heard judgment pronounced against him twice (20:42; 21:20-26), and been granted reprieve (21:27-29). Yet he does not think to seek God's guidance before going to war to recover Ramoth-gilead and scorns Micaiah's message of defeat. The story of Ahab is one of God's determination to win the king which is countered by human vacillation, obtuseness, enmity to God's servants, and defiance of God's word.

The passage teaches that God requires alertness and good judgment in dealing with ambiguous situations. When faced with conflicting messages, each given in the conviction that it is divinely inspired, it does not necessarily follow that the majority report, or the one that coincides with one's own ambitions, is the true one. Above all, it is a futile enterprise to try to outwit the word of a true prophet. God can use those who give assurance of success to bring about judgment. An arrow shot at random can be turned into an instrument of the divine purpose.

SUMMARY AND CONCLUSION
1 Kings 22:39-40

In addition to the standard information for ending the account of a king's reign (see above on 14:21–16:28), Ahab's ivory (paneled) palace and "all the cities" he built are mentioned. The ivory is documented by the discovery of a wealth of carved ivory inlay work at Samaria. While only Jericho is named of the cities Ahab built (16:34), archaeological excavations at Hazor and Megiddo show that he was active there, and this may also be assumed for Samaria. The craftsmanship of Ahab's masons is noteworthy for its excellence. In sheer ability and energy, Ahab belongs to the first rank among Israelite kings.

PART V
AFTER THE DEATH OF AHAB

1 Kings 22:41–2 Kings 8:29

A large block of material beginning at 1 Kgs. 22:41 covers the reigns of Ahab's two sons who succeeded him and the contemporary Judahite kings. Political history is treated skimpily and primarily as a setting for the ministry of Elisha, the dominant personality of these chapters. As a result of the work of Elijah, Elisha, and other prophets, a gradual awakening to the dangers of Canaanite ways and values takes place. As the people return to their Israelite heritage, resentment builds against the house of Ahab until it explodes in the violent revolution of Jehu (2 Kgs. 9–10).

THE REIGN OF JEHOSHAPHAT OF JUDAH (22:41-50)

The focus of 1 Kgs. 22:41–2 Kgs. 8:29 continues to be on the northern kingdom, as it has been since the death of Solomon. Jehoshaphat of Judah is introduced at this point because his reign (870-848 B.C.) provides a dateline for the reigns of Ahab's sons Ahaziah and Joram.

Jehoshaphat is praised for walking "in all the way" of Asa, his father, but faulted (as was Asa) for not doing away with the high places. He is credited in particular with ending the civil war with Israel (1 Kgs. 22:44) and removing what remained of the male cult prostitutes in Judah (v. 46)—evidence of the tenacious hold this practice had gained. Jehoshaphat also built a fleet at Ezion-geber to revive the Red Sea trade initiated by Solomon (9:26-28; 10:22). But the ships he built were wrecked while still in port (22:48), probably because of the ineptness of Judahite shipbuilders and sailors. Ahaziah of Israel offered to enter into partnership in the Red Sea trade, but Jehoshaphat refused (v. 49). Jehoshaphat had access to the Red Sea because "there was no king in Edom" (v. 47) and Judah again exercised control over that country (cf. 11:14-22).

THE REIGN OF AHAZIAH OF ISRAEL (22:51–2 Kgs. 1:18)

The division of the originally single scroll of Kings (introduced by the LXX) at this point severs the introduction to the brief reign of Ahaziah (853-852) from the rest of the account (2 Kgs. 1:1-18).

1 Kings thus ends with the LORD's anger against Ahaziah for continuing the policies of Ahab and Jezebel as well as those of Jeroboam, foreshadowing the terrible consequences of that anger in 2 Kings, an anger that Judah would come to know as well.

SELECTED BIBLIOGRAPHY

Commentaries

Auld, A. Graeme. *I & II Kings*. Daily Study Bible (Philadelphia: Westminster and Edinburgh: Saint Andrew, 1986).

Brueggemann, Walter. *1 Kings*. Knox Preaching Guides (Atlanta: John Knox, 1982).

Burney, C. F. *Notes on the Hebrew Text of the Books of Kings* (1903; repr. New York: KTAV, 1970).

DeVries, Simon J. *1 Kings*. Word Biblical Commentary (Waco: Word, 1985).

Dilday, R. H. *1, 2 Kings*. Communicator's Commentary (Waco: Word, 1987).

Gray, John. *I & II Kings*, 2nd ed. Old Testament Library (Philadelphia: Westminster and London: SCM, 1970).

Jones, G. H. *1 and 2 Kings*, 2 vols. New Century Bible Commentary (Grand Rapids: Eerdmans and London: Marshall, Morgan & Scott, 1984).

Long, Burke O. *1 Kings: with an Introduction to Historical Literature*. Forms of the Old Testament Literature (Grand Rapids: Eerdmans, 1984).

Montgomery, James A. *The Books of Kings*, ed. Henry S. Gehman. International Critical Commentary (Edinburgh: T. & T. Clark and New York: Scribner, 1951).

Nelson, Richard D. *First and Second Kings*. Interpretation (Atlanta: John Knox, 1987).

Noth, Martin. *Könige*. Biblischer Kommentar (Neukirchen-Vluyn: Neukirchener Verlag, 1968).

Patterson, Richard D. and Hermann J. Austel. "1, 2 Kings," in *The Expositor's Bible Commentary*, ed. Frank E. Gaebelein (Grand Rapids: Zondervan, 1988) 4:3-170.

Robinson, Joseph. *The First Book of Kings*. Cambridge Bible Commentary (Cambridge: Cambridge University Press, 1972).

Skinner, John. *I and II Kings*. Century Bible (Edinburgh: T. C. & E. C. Jack, 1904).

Snaith, Norman H. "The First and Second Books of Kings: Introduction and Exegesis," in *The Interpreter's Bible,* ed. George Arthur Buttrick (New York: Abingdon, 1954) 3:1-186.

The Temple

Clements, Ronald E. *God and Temple* (Oxford: Blackwell and Philadelphia: Fortress, 1965).

Endres, John. *Temple, Monarchy and Word of God* (Wilmington: Michael Glazier, 1988).

Garber, Paul L. "Reconstructing Solomon's Temple," *Biblical Archaeologist* 14 (1951): 2-24.

Parrot, André. *The Temple of Jerusalem* (New York: Philosophical Library, 1955, and London: SCM, 1957).

Wright, George Ernest. "Solomon's Temple Resurrected," *Biblical Archaeologist* 4/2 (1941): 17-31.

The Deuteronomistic History

Brueggemann, Walter. "The Kerygma of the Deuteronomistic Historian: Gospel for Exiles," *Interpretation* 22 (1968): 387-402.

Cross, Frank Moore. "The Themes of the Book of Kings and the Structure of the Deuteronomistic History," in *Canaanite Myth and Hebrew Epic* (Cambridge, Mass.: Harvard University Press, 1973), 274-289.

Fretheim, Terence E. *Deuteronomic History*. Interpreting Biblical Texts (Nashville: Abingdon, 1983).

Mayes, A. D. H. *The Story of Israel between Settlement and Exile: A Redactional Study of the Deuteronomistic History* (London: SCM, 1983).

Nelson, Richard D. *The Double Redaction of the Deuteronomistic History* (Sheffield: JSOT Press, 1981).

Noth, Martin. *The Deuteronomistic History*. Journal for the Study of the Old Testament Supplement 15 (Sheffield: JSOT Press, 1979).

von Rad, Gerhard. "The Deuteronomic Theology of History in *I* and *II Kings,*" in *The Problem of the Hexateuch and Other Essays* (1966; repr. London: SCM, 1984), 205-221.

Van Seters, John. *In Search of History: Historiography in the Ancient World and the Origins of Biblical History* (New Haven: Yale University Press, 1983).

Wolff, Hans Walter. "The Kerygma of the Deuteronomic Historical Work," in *The Vitality of Old Testament Traditions,* ed. Walter Brueggemann and Wolff (Atlanta: John Knox, 1975), 83-100.

Articles

Abbott, Nabia. "Pre-Islamic Arab Queens," *American Journal of Semitic Languages and Literatures* 58 (1941): 1-22.

Albright, William F. "The Chronology of the Divided Monarchy of Israel," *Bulletin of the American Schools of Oriental Research* 100 (1945): 16-22.

_____. "Egypt and the Early History of the Negeb," *Journal of the Palestine Oriental Society* 4 (1924): 131-161.

_____. "The Role of the Canaanites in the History of Civilization," in *The Bible and the Ancient Near East,* ed. George Ernest Wright (Garden City: Doubleday, 1961), 328-362.

Cohn, Robert L. "The Literary Logic of 1 Kings 17–19," *Journal of Biblical Literature* 101 (1982): 333-350.

Gross, Walter. "Lying Prophet and Disobedient Man of God in 1 Kings 13: Role Analysis as an Instrument of Theological Interpretation of an OT Narrative Text," *Semeia* 15 (1979): 97-135.

Hansberry, William L. "The Queen of Sheba," in *Pillars in Ethiopian History* (Washington: Howard University Press, 1974), 35-59.

Haran, Menahem. "The Rise and Decline of the Empire of Jeroboam ben Joash," *Vetus Testamentum* 17 (1967): 266-297.

Liver, J. "The Book of the Acts of Solomon," *Biblica* 48 (1967): 75-101.

Mazar, Benjamin. "The Cities of the Priests and the Levites," *Supplements to Vetus Testamentum* 7 (1960): 193-205.

Miller, J. Maxwell. "The Fall of the House of Ahab," *Vetus Testamentum* 17 (1967): 319-324.

Montgomery, James A. "Archival Data in the Book of Kings," *Journal of Biblical Literature* 53 (1934): 46-52.

Napier, B. Davie. "The Omrides of Jezreel," *Vetus Testamentum* 9 (1959): 366-378.

Porten, Bezalel. "The Structure and Theme of the Solomon Narrative (I Kings 3–11)," *Hebrew Union College Annual* 38 (1967): 93-128.

Rowley, H. H. "Elijah on Mount Carmel," *Bulletin of the John Rylands Library* 43 (1960/1961): 190-219. Repr. in *Men of God* (London: Thomas Nelson, 1963), 37-65.

Scott, R. B. Y. "The Pillars of Jachin and Boaz," *Journal of Biblical Literature* 58 (1939): 143-49.

Seale, M. S. "The Black Arabs of the Jordan Valley," *Expository Times* 68 (1956/1957): 28.

Terrien, Samuel L. "The Omphalos Myth and Hebrew Religion," *Vetus Testamentum* 20 (1970): 315-338.

Wenham, John W. "The Black Arabs of the Jordan Valley," *Expository Times* 68 (1956/1957): 121.

General Works

Bright, John. *A History of Israel*, 3rd ed. (Philadelphia: Westminster and London: SCM, 1981).

Felder, Cain Hope. *Troubling Biblical Waters: Race, Class and Family* (Maryknoll, N.Y.: Orbis, 1989).

Hayes, John H. and J. Maxwell Miller, eds. *Israelite and Judean History* (Philadelphia: Westminster and London: SCM, 1977).

Heschel, Abraham J. *The Prophets* (New York: Harper & Row and Jewish Publication Society of America, 1962).

Kitchen, Kenneth A. *The Third Intermediate Period in Egypt* (1100-650 B.C.) (Warminster: Aris and Phillips, 1973).

Newman, Murray L., Jr. *The People of the Covenant: A Study of Israel from Moses to the Monarchy* (Nashville: Abingdon, 1962).

Pedersen, Johannes. *Israel, Its Life and Culture*, I-II (1926; repr. London: Oxford University Press, 1963).

von Rad, Gerhard. *Studies in Deuteronomy*. Studies in Biblical Theology 9 (London: SCM and Chicago: Regnery, 1953).

Simons, J. *The Geographical and Topographical Texts of the Old Testament*. Studia Francisci Scholten 2 (Leiden: Brill, 1959).

Snowden, F. M., Jr. *Blacks in Antiquity: Ethiopians in the Greco-Roman Experience* (Cambridge, Mass.: Harvard University Press, 1970).

Thiele, Edwin R. *The Mysterious Numbers of the Hebrew Kings*, 2nd ed. (Grand Rapids: Wm. B. Eerdmans, 1965).